Sometimes The Bologna Was Fried

Following The Sparrow Tracks

Billy Blackman

Foreword

There are so many ways to experience *Sometimes The Bologna Was Fried*. It can be taken on strictly the story level - reading the surface words that will make you laugh or cry or tilt your head sideways at the funny - almost inexplicable - things the characters do. There is a certain reassurance in these things because we have experienced so many of them ourselves - especially for those of us 'of a certain age' who were raised up in the rural South.

But there is a much deeper level. Billy introduces you to his daddy, a hardworking, God-fearing man of the cloth who could bring his children - his children in every sense of the word - to their feet or to their knees.

Billy had a keen eye as a child, but it took becoming a man to understand the lessons he learned from his daddy. He shares these with us and what a gift that is for his readers. Each story is unique and each story has a different lesson as Aesop might tell it, but together they offer us a delightful journey. You will look in greater depth at the things you remember and see how they fit into what you have become.

Different stories, different influences. But, in the end, these are the things that sculp who we are and there is comfort in that. Our daddies are never really gone. What we choose to do with what they have taught us - most often perhaps unwittingly - shapes our lives and will shape the lives of our children.

Sometimes The Bologna Was Fried makes us take a step backwards to revisit those little things we may have passed over, those things that we may have tucked away in forgotten hidey-holes. If we open our eyes and open our ears, we will hear the rest of the story. We should be grateful for every one of our memories. And we should be grateful for every one of Billy's memories. You will come to know and love his daddy for who he was and you will come to know and love the author for who he has become, and maybe - just maybe - you will come to know yourself a bit better.

Heaven is a rainy day, a comfortable chair, and this book.

— Sue Boyd

Preface

THIS BOOK IS PERSONAL to me.

These stories are a mingle of where I have been and where I'm going—a tangle of life's logbook I can tell about.

If you're wondering where I'm going, well, I guess that depends on your definitions of Heaven and Hell.

This book is about my parents, Woodrow and Kathleen Blackman. It's about my aunts, uncles, grandparents, juke joints, churches, the working class, cats and cousins. It's about hardy guffaws and wannabe outlaws, and honky tonk clowns with fake smiles that hide the real frowns. The pages are an honest reflection of my past.

Much of this book is about my daddy, also known in hallelujah circles as "that preacher man with six fingers on each hand."

I read somewhere that the biblical giant Goliath had six fingers on each hand. Daddy was no giant in the physical sense. By the time I was 16, I was already taller than him. But a guiding light doesn't have to be tall if it's sitting on top of a mountain. God was Daddy's mountain.

I don't remember the exact moment when he was called to preach. It was like at one point he is not a preacher, then he is.

I always knew I was supposed to be a musician. I remember listening to songs on the radio as a child and somehow knowing that a change was about to happen. Later I learned it was a chord change. Maybe Daddy was always supposed to be a preacher. He just didn't know it until after his life went through its chord change during a revival meeting on a ball field in Port St. Joe, Florida.

During the times I traveled, searching for a way through the dark, he was my lighthouse, more by his actions than by his words. His life was a visual, moral code not written on paper, but lived.

This book is part of the story of where he'd been and how that relates to all the turns in the road that led me to where I have ended up.

I hope after reading these pages, a few people might see a little light and come to realize, as I did, how important it is to know where you've been if you want to know where you're going.

With that in mind, I dedicate this book to my 4-year-old grandson, Jude, so that he might one day read it and know from where he came.

-Billy Blackman

Where I've been

WHERE I'M GOING

"IT'S SO DARK OUT here a feller'd have'ta use both hands to find his own fanny."

I wasn't talking to anyone in particular, just mumbling while tripping over a black cat that's always underfoot. She weaves between my feet like a drunk cowboy looking for the front door that just doesn't seem to be where it used to be.

"Dang, Helen! Get outta the way!"

As I was trying to make my way toward the truck, we both danced around like two hogs hung up in a hot wire.

The truck door popped and moaned as I pulled it open. My back protests the same way when I get out of bed every morning. Both the door and my back would benefit from a shot of WD-40. Ninety proof for me.

The ignition switch on the steering column is so worn out that I don't need a key anymore, so it doesn't matter that there's no dome light to guide my aim.

The engine started right up.

The noise coming from under the hood sounded like somebody using a shovel to stir a pot of bolts boiling on a campfire. Smells that way too. I guess that's normal for a work truck with 400,000 miles of experience under its belt. I bought the truck used in 1996. It was only a year old and in good shape. But now it has more dents and holes than a watermelon rind after spending the night in a chicken yard.

We are in the new moon phase, so the predawn is darker than normal. But I still have to back the truck to the barn to load a bale of hay. That way I can throw it out to the horses and get on the road at first light, point my pickup north toward south Georgia and maybe get there before the gnats wake up.

A bucket of warm water sitting in the truck bed is soaking beet pulp pellets for the horses and warming two cans of cat food that are floating in the mix. The water sloshes over the rim as I ease out on the sticky clutch pedal. It grabs, slips, then grabs again.

Henry, Euzema and Calamity are mules that live just across the state line. I have to trim their hooves this morning. My plan is to get there and get it done before the day gets hot and those south Georgia gnats start swarming around my head as if it were a bucket of slop that has been sitting out in the sun too long.

I'm a self-employed farrier. If I don't work, I don't eat. And if you ever gazed upon my girth, you'd conclude that I must work a lot.

Last week was busy and my 72-year-old body is protesting. There was a time when the day would run out of light long before my legs ran out of gas. Now it's the opposite. Now by sundown, I'm grunting so much that I could be mistaken for a "hog whisperer."

No matter. The work has to be done. As the ole folks used to say, "pity won't feed the bulldog."

Backing my truck up to the barn would be easier if I had more daylight or better tail lights. It's a leap of faith, this backing through the darkness. Helen or the other cats could be back there somewhere.

Fifty years ago, if you had told me I would one day care one iota if I bumped into a cat while backing my truck, I would have wondered what you were drinking.

But here I am, soaking two cans of cat food in heated water so five cats can have a warm breakfast.

I say five cats, but, as far as holding titles to and owning outright, we have only three. I'm also counting two loafering toms that don't belong to anybody. They just stop by the barn most mornings for a handout.

For the sake of the tranquility of the countryside, I can only hope they show up at different times.

Since the older grey tabby tom has been mooching here for over two years, we assigned him a name, "Mason - The Traveling Man."

The other tom is much younger and a recent stopover whom we've yet to name. The wife calls him "that orange cat" in the same tone she uses when she talks about a full garbage can that's stinking and needs to be dumped into the big can outside.

Warm up a cat's breakfast? I never would have done that fifty years ago—not even ten years ago.

Mason looks like he has had a rough life.

On some days he limps around like a bar bouncer on a Sunday morning. When I see Mason limping, I'll crumble up pain medicine and sprinkle it on his food.

To be so old, he can still handle himself pretty good during territorial tumblings with "that orange cat."

The ritual never changes when those two cross paths on their way to the barn buffet. They stop and give each other hypnotic, icy stares for a few seconds. But that's just the opening ceremony before the cat chaos. Then it starts, and it gets loud. Next it rains cats without the dogs. The flying hair and growls add sound and visual effects to a perfect storm of cat cussing and acrobatics. It looks and sounds like both are stuck in a spin/dry cycle of a catawampus Maytag.

The last I heard of them, they were spooking birds and disrupting the tranquility as they tumbled north toward Bainbridge.

By the next day, "that orange cat" was off loafering again like most young guns do. Mason was limping around the yard thinking he'd won, and I was looking for his pill bottle.

I'm also moving slow this morning, inside my truck while turtling backwards in the dark toward a barn I hope to see before I back into it.

There's always a chance there might be a cat or two behind me somewhere. So I stay ready to stomp the brake, in case I bump into something that sounds furry, even if it's two toms stuck in a spin/dry cycle.

There are no backup lights and just one tail light working on this "been there - done that" Ford. I busted them out years ago, so I can see nothing behind me. The back bumper is supposed to protect the lights. But it's too bent up to protect much of anything. It's had too many encounters with fence posts, trees, and other solid objects that have a tendency to jump out in front of me when I'm backing up.

Through the rearview mirror, I can't see where I'm going. But I can see where I've been through the dusty windshield, thanks to a pair of dustier headlights. Well, kinda see anyway, in a dim lit-dimwit-misfit sort of way.

I figure it would help if I gave the headlights—well, all the truck—a good scrubbing. But I'm reluctant to wash anything.. The dirt clods might be holding hands and I don't want to disturb that comradery of mud and rust. It might be all that's holding the bumper on.

Despite the headlight grime, there is just enough light to see by, especially against such a pitch-black backdrop. Out here it's a complete darkness only rural areas can produce in places where streetlights have yet to intrude.

In front of me I can see the old oak out near the road. When I line up the headlights with it, that means the barn door is directly behind me. Even though I can't see it, I know it's there.

Even the bugs are trying to help guide me. It's mid-summer and I see fireflies flickering on and off in the blackness that envelops everything except what my headlights manage to mitigate. The fireflies aren't much help, but I appreciate any help I can get, even if it is low wattage.

Their flickering reminds me of a honky tonk dance floor so dark that you can't see the people. But you know they are there because of occasional flickering as they light up their Camels and Marlboros—foil packs of non-filtered fireflies that nest inside sweat-stained shirt pockets.

This morning, the fireflies flicker in tune with a melody that I cannot hear. During such early start mornings, the lonely moan of the train blowing at the Midway crossing two miles away is about the only sound out here. Well, the only sound I can hear, anyway. I'm sure that surrounding me is the same acoustical jigsaw puzzle that was there before my ears went bad: frogs, bees, bats, locusts, and the low grunt of a bullfrog in the swamp a hundred yards away.

All the audible puzzle pieces are here. I just can't hear them because of the constant, play-along crickets ringing bells in my ears and drowning out everything else. Too many years of standing in front of screaming amps will do that.

But what I can hear is a familiar radio voice coming from the speaker behind the truck dash. It's that old prophet-for-profit broadcasting his radio show out of Macon, Georgia. He's the same preacher I used to listen to late nights while driving home from a gig. I found him this morning while searching stations for steel guitars. His tactics haven't changed. His is still the voice inside my dash who I think needs to alter his path to the altar. He is the reverend of irreverence who is not awe-filled, but just plain aw-ful. He is a lamb on the lam, a trader in nonsense for cents.

For many years he has been bringing home the bacon live from Macon. I'm a little surprised he's still at it.

I know his MO. I've smelled that kind of frying and lying before. He is about to ask me to lay my hands on the dash so he can pray with me. Then in a few seconds he'll ask me to put that same hand in my pocket to send him $20, along with my prayer request. But if I'm in a hurry to get my prayers answered, then send $50. When asking for money, he was then and still is as subtle as a bale of hay falling off a truck.

When compared to one six-fingered, genuine man of God I grew up watching and listening to, well, the radio preacher just doesn't have the same wattage.

A guy once asked that six-fingered preacher why he didn't charge a fee for preaching.

"I cain't and I ain't gonna charge for that," he said. "It's the Lord's work."

This six-fingered preacher was my daddy, Woodrow Blackman—the "real deal," an authentic man of God.

When I was playing jukes and traveling home late at night, I guess I listened to that radio preacher because I was looking for the "real deal," but wound up listening to somebody wanting to steal. I didn't realize it at the time, but I was searching for an off ramp to get me out of the bars. My life was looking more and more like the fading center line on that "Lost Highway" Hank Sr. sang about.

Mama had already warned me how the road to Heaven and the road to Hell looked a lot alike, except for that one fork in the road. She always prayed that I wouldn't take the wrong fork and end up spoon-feeding the devil. Her prayers went unanswered. I ended up playing music every night but Sundays, trying to drive people to drink. In contrast, Daddy would whoop and holler, dance in place, speak in tongues and try to drive a few of those same people back to the Lord. It was like I had opened the gate and he was trying to shut it.

This morning, the dashboard preacher sounded more pathetic than prophetic when he said, "I have been all over this world preaching the gospel. I've traveled thousands of miles for God. And some of y'all won't even cross the street to mail me $20 so I can ask God to help you. Can I get a witness?"

Believe me, I'm as close to being a Bible scholar as a baby rattler is to being a baby rattle. But in this continuing journey from "last call" to "altar call," I've been around long enough to recognize charlatan from Shinola, and that old familiar voice inside my dash is shining the people and not their shoes.

I'd heard it all before. So I turned off the distraction and, without the sounds of the man from Macon trying to get me to pay for his bacon, I continued my slow journey backwards toward the barn.

The ole folks at home came to mind again: "Sometimes it's hard to see sump'um if you don't know what you're a'looking fer. It's also hard to be lost if you don't know where you're s'pose to be."

Well, this morning I know what I'm looking for—the hay room door, and I know where I'm supposed to end up—just short of backing into it.

With the oak tree lined up in my dusty light sights, I am where I'm supposed to be as I start this journey backwards.

I am on the path to my reward, if you consider a bale of hay a reward. I give the oak a quick glimpse before the headlights abandon it, just to make sure I am still in line with the hay room door.

With the Confederate Rose out front and to the left, the peach limb out front and to the right, I continue to snail backwards, looking to the left again and waiting for the first lighted glimpse of the fig tree. When I see it, I will know that the barn is only a few feet behind me.

"There it is."

I mash in the clutch and roll to a stop at the place where memory has delivered me and where knowledge begins, the knowledge that I am now where I am supposed to be, and I got here because I could see where I'd been.

It's not easy to get lost in the dark between a peach tree and a Confederate Rose. But it can happen if you don't have at least a little light to go by.

Even at my age, I still sometimes wonder where I'm going. So I rely on the history of my people to show me where I have been so I will know where I'm going and maybe keep myself from getting lost along the way—for very long, anyway. After all, we're just stumbling around in the dark, tripping over black cats and that one fork in the road while trying to find our way to Heaven or, in my case this morning, the hay room door.

Breathing

HELL WITH THE FIRES OUT

STANDING UNDER MY FAMILY tree and shaking it could be dangerous. A pulpit, a guitar amp or a bottom plow might fall out and hit you on your head.

Those genetics are why I was destined to go into one of three lines of work: preaching, music, or farming. I call it the trinity of destiny: homily, harmony, or hominy. But no matter the vocation of my people, they had a long sweaty relationship with elbow grease.

As a class, they had sore backs and a belief that with a little education and a lot of help from God, their children wouldn't have to plow behind a deadhead mule or pick down endless cotton rows that stretched beyond their future, stretched past quitting time, or maybe even stretched as far as the end of time.

Most of that lineage had clean hearts wrapped in sweat-stained cotton shirts. The men wore faded overalls the color of a bluebird winter sky and the women wore dresses that still smelled a little like chicken feed. The hide on the backs of their necks was raw and cracked like an over-baked biscuit... the same color, too. Calluses on their hands were as tough as a twice-fried pork chop. Blisters had burst and healed over many times. Those calluses were so gizzard-tough that if one of my ancestors had turned out to be our savior, the Romans would have had a hard time driving a spike through it and nailing him to a post.

This was a sweaty, genetic group. They carried wax paper wrapped bologna sandwiches to the job inside empty syrup buckets and later inside metal lunch pails. Most of them were as honest as a bathroom mirror at 4 AM, so cheating you out of a penny was as foreign to them as a hundred-dollar bill.

They were stubborn, proud, stoop-labor stock, the sort of people where the surest way to get them to do a job that nobody else could or would do was to tell them they couldn't get it done. And when it came to getting it done, they could do most anything: fix their own flats, nail on their own shingles, doctor their wounds with kerosene and bandage them in prayer requests. Some had their pictures made shaking hands with the sheriff, while others had their picture made handcuffed to the door handle of the sheriff's car. They were a diverse bunch of kin folks, a hardworking bunch who knew that life was no gravy train and that work boots ain't made of biscuits.

They knew at some point that everybody was going to stumble and fall—unless you were a snake. When that happened, they didn't stay on the ground. They got back up and took care of whatever needed taking care of.

They knew how to sharpen their own pocket knives and chainsaws, and they knew how to repack a wheel bearing on a boat trailer. They could tune up their own skipping cars and nail shoes on their own sore-footed horses. And on the morning of the first frost, they knew how to go out to the hog pen with a .22 rifle and a butcher knife and take care of business, while making their young'uns wait in the house because survival ain't always pretty and sometimes involves blood. They could make cracklin' bread and hog head cheese, and put a little spice and vinegar in that and turn it into something different called "souse." And they would fight you in a second if you even hinted that 'rasselin' and Jesus weren't real. They could tell you the best time to plant peas, and in what months you are not supposed to eat oysters, but they couldn't tell you why. "Jes cause that's what Daddy said," they'd say with authority. Some of them knew the chant to make warts go away and believed in the healing powers of snuff fresh from a bottom lip. And it didn't have to be a preacher's bottom lip, either. They stood for the flag, kneeled for the cross, and could dig wigglers and bait a hook. They could skin a catfish and kill a snake with a rusty hoe, its handle held together with electrician's tape because a good hoe handle is worth the effort. And they would threaten to hit you over the head with a Bible if you even hinted that it is okay to fish on a Sunday.

To Daddy and his generation and the ones before them, the code was simple: if you could work and feed your babies but wouldn't, then you were the lowest form of life, hovering along the bottom with liars, mudcats and stink jims. Or in a worse case, a Republican.

"And if a man will lie to you," his generation believed, "that man will steal your chickens to fry up and feed the people he invites to his political rally."

Most of the time, they were right because they mostly were so honest that a preacher could rest easy playing poker with them over the telephone. That is, if they'd had telephones.

Daddy's work was important not only to him, but to an entire generation who was defined by what they did with their hands—the pulp wooders and painters, the farmers and factory workers.

They were a group where pride in the job they did was just as important as the dollars they got paid for doing it.

It was in their genes. They couldn't help being that way. It was as natural to them as breathing.

It seems this magnitude of importance they attached to work could be passed on from generation to generation, like blue or brown eyes, the talent to play and sing and preach, or the unexplainable love of snuff, whiskey, and fried chicken.

It didn't matter what they were doing, as long as they were doing something. Some of their children were the same way.

I guess that lineage is why I feel like I always have to be working on something, on anything. I guess that genetic pool still had water in it when I was born — along with a few liars, mudcats and stink jims. But no Republicans.

To me, working is as much a part of life as, well... breathing.

You could tell it was spring in North Florida—two days ago it was 45 degrees when the sun came up. This morning it was already 75 and the sun had not even shown up for work yet. But a working man needed no light to know that he was already tired from wading through pine tops left by yesterday's efforts. As he walked toward where he'd stopped the day before, he had a chainsaw on his shoulder, a gas can in one hand, a plastic water jug tied to his belt loop and nothing in his pockets except for a Case knife and a red sweat rag.

At one time, he carried the gas in a glass jug with a finger hole near the spout. Then one day he accidentally set the woods on fire. He had left the jug out in the sun and the sunlight shining through the glass focused its attention on a clump of grass behind it. Any Boy Scout with a magnifying glass will tell you that's all it takes to start a fire. The government had already decreed "no more glass bottles of gasoline in the woods." But how would a fellow in Washington know the difference in the price of a glass jug from the trash and a gas can from the hardware store?

The working man knew from experience that as the day progressed, even though it was only spring, it would get so hot that the sun would seem to move slower and slower across the sky in its amble toward dusk, the cooler part of the day. So the last thing he needed was something else to heat up his world, like a grass fire. What little breeze that did blow was as hot as the air it rode in on. The humidity had already outpaced the temperature as if they were in a race to see which could soak him down first.

As the sun rose, the sky was a smoky blue and the air as thin and damp as the sweaty cotton T-shirt he was wearing. The rattlesnakes, yellow jackets, red bugs, the ticks in the woods and the bankers in town all waited on bad luck to give them a shot at a working man walking by. Then, to add a little vinegar to the wounds, the chainsaw wouldn't start, and the pulpwood truck was still hung up on a stump from yesterday's run in with bad luck.

But that really didn't matter much today because the paper mill had already sent word that they would be cutting his quota this week. And it was only Tuesday. But he is too stubborn to slow down because the reality of a situation is sometimes hard to see when you have so much sweat in your eyes. Plus, he couldn't stop because he had mouths back home to feed.

But he did stop for a moment after he found a stump in the shade, a mildly cooler place where he could set down to work on the chainsaw, to catch his breath, rest his back and to wipe some sweat with a rag already overworked and over-damp.

We all have our own ways of getting backaches, and this was his. But when you mix backache with heartache—well, in that case, no matter which way you look, the view never changes. And what ached his heart was the thought that back home, in a Jim Walter house that belonged to somebody else, the rent, the light bill and the wife were all past due—again.

But he was not alone in this bog of melancholy. Back at the house, his wife's heart hurt, too. It ached when she looked out the window, hoping to see good luck coming up the driveway. Instead, what she saw was their car parked on a hill so they could push it off to start. The battery was bad and, like gas cans, a good battery costs dollars, and dollars were as scarce as a week when the mill didn't cut your quota.

Out in the piney woods, he was doing all he could do to change that, and a better life was always just around the next pile of pine tops. But they were both weary of the "worse" mentioned in the wedding vows. What about the "better?" When was it gonna show up?

He was sure that some people around town used him as an example to their children of what they would become if they did not get a proper, store-bought education. Those people thought of him and his family as "trash." He remembered what his mama once told a lady in a store who called her—and everybody who went to her church—"trash."

"Well," Mama said, "at least trash floats on top."

Floating on top was about all this working man could manage right now. He was sweating every day to keep his head just far enough out of the water not to drown in a lake called "Just Get'n By."

But with a wife who has more faith and confidence in him than he has in himself, a man can do almost anything he sets his mind to. And he surely had that kind of wife.

He called her "sugar plum," even when they were arguing over rent money and diapers.

Even while sitting on the stump in a sweaty shirt, you might say he had thoughts of Christmas because he had visions of "sugar plum" dancing in his head. The experts call it the Christmas emotion, the expectation of better things to come.

This would be their third child and one of the "things to come" that kept him going. His daddy told him once that some men never grow up until they have babies to feed. "And some don't even do it then," his daddy had said. Those words stuck with him, so he took care of his family. Not doing that would be the "ultimate sin."

He was only 25 years old, but it seems he has been an adult all of his life. He was already tired. Even the old chainsaw had the advantage over him because it got to break down sometimes and, in doing so, got to rest. He could not afford to breakdown or to rest, not for very long, anyway.

The only rest he'd have that day would come between the first and second loads of wood, a brief span of time allotted to eat a bite of dinner. The metal lunchbox he brought with him from home had a dent in one side. His head put that crease in the side after he once used the lunch bucket as a pillow during a rare nap. Inside the lunchbox were two egg sandwiches and a slab of pound cake leftover from Sunday, a sweetened antidote from the "Day of Rest," devoted to the half-day of work left to do.

But there was one thing that this type work had taught him—that if he ever got a "good" job and felt the need to bellyache about it, he could just think on where he had been, and the ache would probably just go away.

But what would not "just go away" was the reality that his chainsaw wouldn't start. No running chainsaw meant no wood on the ground. No wood on the ground meant no money in his pocket. No money in his pocket meant no food on the table.

He unscrewed the spark plug from the saw so he could clean it and dip the firing end in gas as a sort of booster shot, then screwed it back in. As he worked on the saw, he looked around at a landscape distorted and dancing in the heat waves, and he talked to himself, which is the most intimate and honest of all conversations any of us will ever have.

"This has got to be what hell would look like if they ever get the fires put out," he said.

Then he glanced to the right and saw a distant sign, tilted and hanging on a pine tree. He squinted his eyes, wiped the sweat from his forehead, stood up and walked toward the sign. Still squinting, with his head tilted at the same angle as the sign, he tried to read the words.

Finally he is close enough to read it: "GET SAVED OR ELSE THE DEVIL IS COMING TO GET YOU AND WILL TAKE YOU STRAIGHT TO HELL!"

"Well," he said to himself, mildly amused while mildly serious, as if challenging the Devil himself. "Come on, if you're coming. Anywhere has got to be better than this!"

Fear of that place where preachers seem to want to send him is not what drives him to take care of his family. He has not committed that "ultimate sin." Nope, he is driven by some inner force that neither he, nor his daddy, nor his daddy's daddy understood. Like breathing, it had always been there, this willingness, almost passion for work. To him it was a booster seat he'd sat on even when he was too little to reach the big table where the menfolk sat around and smoked as much as the chainsaws they ran, and that ran them.

Unafraid, he turned and walked back to the stump and to his chainsaw, put the wire back on the spark plug, and gave the crank cord a snatch. It started!

And he went back to work. He went back to breathing.

Hard Times

EAT'N CHICKEN FEET

SOMEWHERE UNDER SOMETHING, I have a picture of Daddy standing with his brothers and sister. He looks to be around nine years old. All of them look as ragged and wore out as a porkchop bone that has done time in a dog pen. Life had already chewed on them pretty hard.

Though the picture is in black and white, in my mind I can see the south Alabama clay they are standing on. The dirt is the color of a rooster's comb and smelled like the floor mat at Heaven's front door. They are all barefooted except for one, and they all look fed but still hungry. No one ever mentioned just where that one pair of shoes came from, and I was too busy and forgot to ask Daddy.

It was around 1930 and word was just trickling south about what people called the "stock market crash." But to the Blackman family, a stock market crash meant something different. The Blackman definition was more like when a rogue bull jumps through the fence at the annual fairground cattle sale, not a man jumping out of a high-rise window because he was afraid to face poverty. Daddy and his brothers were already walking around in overalls with the seats worn thin from age. It seems they were born with hoe-handle blisters already on their fingers and poverty caked between their toes. To them, more hard times were just more of the same stuff they had learned to live with. Kind of like a heat wave in August or mosquitos after dark.

I'm sure that by the time the Blackman children lined up for that picture, their daddy—my grandpa—was already showing signs of what we speculate was the cancer that soon killed him. People said Dan Blackman lay in his bloody bed and screamed from the pain. I doubt a doctor ever saw him. Doctors cost money, and to them money was as rare as a cotton field owner who didn't try to cheat workers out of a pound or two of work every Friday.

Daddy never talked much about his daddy but said once that Grandpa Blackman did like to split firewood.

It was also said that God gifted Dan Blackman with a knack for splitting knotty wood that nobody else volunteered to spend time, pain or muscle on—you know, kinda like finding a volunteer when it comes time to give a cat a bath.

Grandpa had a knack for knots, along with a mule stubbornness to not let some knot stand between his family and the fireplace. He also had the experience of knowing that to split any knot, or any problem you might encounter, you don't have to hit it hard, just hit it in the same place every time.

Daddy's mother, Janie, was a powerful woman of Irish descent. It was good she had that Irish stubborn streak and a strong back because she was already having to take on more of the workload because of her weakening husband. People who knew her said she could pick up and carry a 200 pound sack of feed easier than most men could. Both had to be as tough as sunbaked barbed wire, because even before he got sick, chiseling a living out of dirt as dry as a sawdust sandwich had to be a lot like carving General Lee's horse into Stone Mountain with a cheap pocket knife. I wish I had known her—Grandpa Blackman, too. Both died before I was born.

I never knew hard times like that. We never had to say grace over a pot of boiled poke and chicken necks. Daddy talked about his childhood some, but not much. I guess he was trying to spare us, or trying not to appear to be a braggart for overcoming it. Maybe he was just trying to forget.

As we all do, I wish now I had asked more questions. It's different when the somebody telling the story is the one who wrestled with it and won even though it was a daily battle because poverty pitched a tent and homesteaded right on their doorsteps.

As a generation removed, I might look back on them as "good ol' days." He saw them as not so good!

"When I was a'grow'n up the only thang left hangin' from a hawg that didn't get eat was the squeal," he'd say.

I believe that if hard times had lasted a little longer, they would have figured out how to eat that, too.

But that was long ago and time dulls just about everything, except maybe the memory of a gnawing stomach. It takes cornbread to dull that!

Most little boys look up to their daddies for a lot of reasons. I looked up to mine not only because he overcame the grip of poverty that could have choked the life right out of him if he'd bowed to it, but also because he treated people right and danced and spoke in tongues when the Holy Ghost grabbed him just right. I thought he could have walked on water if good luck had just given him a running start. Or maybe, just maybe, with a little help from on high, he might have been able to turn a hoe handle into a snake, like the Bible talks about.

I got a glimpse of what his young life might have been like when I was ten years old and we were visiting Mama's people in Alabama. We were all seated around the table as a wood stove glowed red just one room away. With the blessing said and the amen over, we were about to eat when I glanced over at Daddy's plate. And I had an epiphany after I saw what was there. A man who will eat fried chicken feet has seen his and somebody else's share of hard times.

My People

18 x 19 x 20

MY PEOPLE WERE NOT from Florida. They were from south Alabama.

Calling them rich would have been stretching the truth so tight a mule could have used it for a trampoline.

Borrowed houses rented from landowners are where most of them lived, near plowed fields they did not own. There they worked crops on halves, their half seeming to never amount to much more than food and rent.

Those tenant houses, as comedian Pigmeat Markham used to say, were 18 x 19 x 20. That wasn't referring to size. That meant if you didn't have $18 by the 19th, you had to be out by the 20th.

Men of that generation, and of that place in time, walked endless miles behind mindless mules as weary as they were, ploughing row after row of red dirt in places like Coffee County,, Alabama, where I was born in 1951.

It was 1952 when Daddy left one borrowed house in south Alabama and moved his young family into another borrowed house in North Florida. He did that because "gettin' by" there had to be easier than "gettin' by" where they were. It just had to be!

Some might say that took a lot of courage.

Courage has nothing to do with it when you're already at the bottom of a hole and there's only one rope dangling down.

For Daddy, fate tied the other end of the rope to the paper mill in Port St. Joe, Florida, and it hoisted him farther away from the bottom than he ever dreamed possible.

But not without a price.

In that mill is where he did literally work himself to death, surrounded by and breathing in decades of flesh-eating paper mill haze that could eat the metal bumpers off cars.

That haze seemed to be full of razor blades and battery acid as it ate up his lungs the same way it ate the paint off his lunch pail. It created even more havoc later on in other parts of Daddy's body and life.

I guess he figured that was the price he had to pay to feed his family. He never complained and gladly put on his old brogans every morning and went to work because there are no briar-less paths to payday.

The mill was a dangerous place to work. The machines could take your finger, your arm or even your life. As far as your life was concerned, it could take it all at once or take it a little at a time—a long process that usually started with a cough. After 40 years of breathing that haze, doctors compared Daddy's lungs to swiss cheese because they had more holes than the roof of a rent-to-own house trailer.

The mill also gave life—as weekly paychecks, paid vacations, insurance, a retirement plan and a chance for the next generation to never have to walk behind a mule again.

That good job also enabled workers to buy in small monthly installments their lawn mowers at the furniture store and their washing machines at the hardware store.

My folks, and almost everybody else of that time, came from tough working stock.

Life defined them not by social status but by their work and a plow-mule determination that just wouldn't allow them to give up.

Give out, yes. Give up, no... you rested and started work again. Then you rested again, got up again and went back to work again because there are negative economic consequences if you don't get out of bed and put on your britches.

They were a self-reliant bunch who believed charity was for giving, not receiving.

The carryover from that independence could be seen in the number of home gardens. Patches of collards and corn sprouted around small houses not borrowed anymore, but owned outright, or one day would be, thanks to Jim Walter financing and paper mill paychecks.

It's true that the home-grown products of your labor taste better and are better for you. But I think the real reason they continued to hoe and hope was because of a fear flowing deep in their very being, a genetic memory that hard times can sometimes be only a payday away.

Those ancestors could do almost anything because nobody else was going to do it for them.

They could nail on shingles and sink roofing nails with one dead-on blow from a hammer, and they knew how to use a sharp pocket knife to make a barrow out of a boar.

They could balance and bounce toddlers on one knee while balancing a plate of peas on the other knee and never drop either. Never! And with hard, callused hands, they could touch that same baby's forehead to check for a fever.

They ate gravy made from coffee, flour and bacon grease, and on special occasions, sometimes the bologna was fried.

Some worked for God and could preach a dead relative into heaven at his funeral, or at least make the family think that was where he was going. Those family members felt relief, despite the rumors that the relative might have been shot for his beliefs. No, not his religious beliefs, but for his belief that it was okay to date a married woman.

Of course, that never happened in my family, at least not that I heard of. But it could have.

Some of them could sling scriptures like green cotton bolls and thump you on the head with a Moses quote from Deuteronomy. Others could moan Hank Sr. songs over a cheap microphone in smoky dance halls with the same tones of struggle and heartbreak as Hank himself.

To them, there were only two books of any importance. In the house, it was the Bible. In the outhouse, it was the Sears catalog,

If you were a man who wouldn't take care of your family, they looked at you with the same suspicion they might look upon a de-scented polecat. You know, the skunk can't do you any harm, but you just never feel at ease being around them.

They had spent their lives working hard and had no respect for anyone who could but did not do the same. "You see that there feller right there," one might say to the others as one of the lowlifes walks by. "That there is the sorriest thang God ever wrapped in hide."

Work is all they knew and work is what they measured other men by.

And the women worked even harder.

They got up early every morning to make breakfast and sandwiches for lunch buckets, then got husbands off to work and kids up, dressed, fed and fluffed for school.

They picked peas and okra and squash while the dew was still on the ground. While they watched the stories on TV, they shelled black-eyed and Cream 40 peas. They shucked and scraped corn to "put up" for the hard times still haunting their sleep.

Later, they would meet with other church ladies to talk about selling bottles of vanilla flavoring and baking pies because a growing church always had a "Building Fund" that needed feeding.

Then they'd go home and start rolling pie crusts with a floured tea glass and start baking until the kids got home from school. Then they'd help with mild math and call out spelling words. "You go lick that calf over and study them words some more and we'll try again later," they'd say.

"Lick that calf over" was always a puzzling phrase to me. I didn't know where it came from, but I knew what it meant. I turned out to be an expert at doing things over again because the first try just wasn't good enough.

By then it was time for the mamas to start supper because menfolk would be home soon, their stomachs growling and their clothes smelling like sweat and paper mill progress.

Then, from a nail driven halfway into the kitchen wall, the women pulled down an iron skillet and started cooking.

In some ways, that old iron skillet had it better than most women. After supper it would get washed and hung back on the wall where it could rest until morning.

Women didn't get the same chance. Spelling words still had to be called out.

Beliefs

SPIT'N ON A FROG

My ancestors, that is since the 1700s anyway, drifted south from the Carolinas, bringing certain beliefs that flowed downhill with them all the way to south Alabama and from there to North Florida.

Many of those beliefs were alive and well to my generation because of a carryover from our parents. I think we believe them because they believed them.

Despite there being no divining rods hanging in our pump houses, my people still put some store in the pseudoscience of superstitions.

For example:

If the sun is shining during a rain shower, then "that ole devil's a'beatin' his wife." And if it's thundering too, that means they are knocking over the furniture.

If you wash your hair during the first rain shower in May, it will grow faster.

Eating black-eyed peas on New Year's Day will bring you good luck, but only if there's some hog jowls cooked in with them. But whatever you do, don't never-ever wash clothes on that day or else that's all you'll be doing all year.

Never sweep dirt out the door after sundown. You might sweep someone out of your life.

And, if you suddenly shiver, that means a possum is walking on the ground where one day you will be buried.

Biddies hatched in May just won't lay and could go blind.

Bottles hanging in your neighbor's tree means he's catching evil spirits. Once caught, he'll put the lid back on the bottle and throw it into the river. A mirror by your front door will chase away any evil spirits that sneak past the bottles.

If a snapping turtle bites you, you can shake your hand and even cut off his head, but he will not let go until it thunders.

If your nose itches, then company is coming. If your feet itch, you'll walk on strange ground. But if the palm of your hand itches, you'll be coming into some unexpected money.

Lord, how much cash have I washed down the drain because ignorant me just thought my itchy hands needed a good scrubbing?

They believed it was bad luck to bring a hoe into the house—although I remember no one ever doing that or why they might even want to. If you do it by mistake, there was an antidote. You simply carried it out backwards through the same door. That reverses the bad luck.

My ancestors believed you could count the number of chirps by a cricket in one minute and that would tell you what the temperature was—although it wasn't all that important to know the exact temperature, other than it was hot or cold.

From experience, they believed it was a waste of time and seed potatoes to plant them any other time except during the dark of the moon.

They believed it would bring good luck if you could trick a doodlebug out of its hole by taking a small stick and stirring it in the hole, while chanting, "Doodlebug, doodlebug, your house is on fire."

My ancestors believed that dipping snuff was a sin and doing so would land you in hell—unless it was Granny Martin you were talking about. God made an exception for her because she was so good and kind that when she walked in the garden, flowers would sprout up in her footprints. In His eyes, her dipping snuff was more of a weakness than it was a sin. Kind of like when the preacher gets a third piece of fried chicken. St. Peter probably handed her a spit can as she skipped across that pearly threshold.

People in my lineage believed it would make it rain if you killed a snake and left its belly pointed toward the sky.

"Frogs will give you warts," they believed. All you had to do to rid yourself of those warts was to put rocks in a sock, the number of rocks matching the number of warts you had, tie a knot in the sock and throw it back over your right shoulder into the bushes, then walk away. Whatever you do, don't look back or even think about it. If you do that, the spell won't work. You know, it would jinx it, like when you tell someone what you wished for after you blow out the birthday candles.

They believed Jesus didn't need to smell your breath to know if you'd been drinking and that you never swept on New Year's Day because, if you do, you might sweep someone you love out of your life.

They all knew that you never castrated an animal during a full moon. Do that then and the animal might bleed to death because blood flows freer during this moon phase.

They believed that finding an honest politician was as rare as finding a skunk in a good mood.

They believed that a good Baptist would go to Heaven just like a Holiness, only the Baptist would be at the end of the line.

Spitting on a dead frog brought you good luck.

If your right eye itched, you were going to get pleased. If your left one itched, you were going to get mad.

They believed in their children.

But they also believed that it was a sin to love your child too much. If you did, a jealous God might take him or her away from you.

As far as I know, loving her children in excess was the only sin my mama was ever guilty of, and in severity that would rank alongside of Granny's snuff dipping.

People Of The Mill

PASSING IT DOWN

MANY OF THEM MOVED their families to the Florida Panhandle from Alabama and Georgia after word of work drifted north.

They brought with them not much more than old shotguns and older Bibles, future heirlooms of sorts. They had little more to bring other than that—and a mule-headed spirit that just wouldn't allow them to give up, no matter what.

They moved to the Florida Panhandle even though the future there was an unknown. But it was still better than the known future where they were coming from. That status quo consisted of plowing somebody else's field behind a brain-dead, borrowed mule and weather as unpredictable as the mule they plowed. That wasn't much to leave behind.

No doubt some were also running from the cotton mills, where paltry paychecks came with the promise of lint-filled lungs and a retirement plan that bolstered a shortened life.

Life for them had been mostly sweaty shirts and drought and had broken just about everything about them except their fighting spirit.

Moving to a new life had to be a fearful time for them. The unknown usually is.

Many of them came in the late 1940s and early 50s, leaving behind all they'd ever known, searching for a life better than the one they'd left behind in Alabama.

Whatever awaited them in North Florida had to be better. It just had to be!

It drew them to places like Honeyville, Dalkeith, Wewahitchka (Wewa for short) and White City, as word drifted north across the state line, rumors that the paper mill in Port St. Joe was hiring. And if the mill thing didn't work out, there were other jobs too, like pulpwooding, logging and even railroad work.

But a mill job was the prize they grabbed for, because a mill job offered them steady work so they could feed their babies. It offered a decent paycheck every week, health insurance, paid vacation and a pension plan. Things like that you don't find between cotton rows, not even on a payday.

Not only that, the mill might make it possible for many of them to make payments on a brand new

Jim Walter house and a like-new Chevrolet. You just never could tell. They might just be that blessed.

Boy howdy, then they could hold their heads up high with a new dignity that many of them never had known.

There were Baptist and Methodist, Presbyterian and Holiness, a variety of beliefs because the working class never had just one religious preference. They all wanted to get to Heaven. It didn't matter to them which mule they were riding.

Many of them, like my parents, ended up in the quiet community of Wewahitchka, Florida, more or less a mill town located twenty-four miles north of Port St. Joe.

When Daddy got there with Mama and 16-month-old me, he had just enough education to sign his name. He had enough math skills to keep from being cheated. And he knew how to paint, at least that's what he told the hiring man in St. Joe. I guess that did the trick because a paper mill built next to salt water needed a lot of painting.

Some folks got to the area already equipped with enough education to be schoolteachers, bankers, and lawyers.

Although many of them spent little time between the cotton rows, their mamas and daddies did. This gave most everyone in Wewahitchka during that time a commonality, whether it was a diploma or a pair of faded overalls hanging on a nail.

Life had never been a barn dance for any of them since they all came up during the Depression.

Sometimes this new life of canned biscuits and store-bought eggs wasn't so easy either. The market for paper goes down sometimes, and so do the mills.

But these "people of the mill" were all as tough as a nickel steak and as gritty as a dropped biscuit. They had the courage of a Piney Woods Rooter—that's a wild hog that lives in the North Florida swamps—and the tenacity of a yellow jacket jarred from his nap by a lawnmower.

There is a recipe for cooking a Piney Woods Rooter: You drop the hog along with a horseshoe in a scalding kettle filled with water. Build a fire and boil until the horseshoe gets tender. Then you can eat the hog.

That's just how that generation was, too. They had to be that way.

Sad, but they and others like them have mostly disappeared now.

At least, I thought they had.

On October 10, 2018, Hurricane Michael, along with its 160 mile-per-hour winds, bulldozes onshore and stomps its way inland, stripping these little communities as clean as a fried chicken platter at a church picnic. Wewa was not spared.

As I rode down the roads there in stunned disbelief at the destruction, I heard the chainsaws and tractors and saw people doctoring their lives and the communities back together again. In them I saw the descendants of the "people of the mill," those babies and the children of those babies now grown.

When you see that, you realize that the toughness, the grittiness, the courage and the tenacity have been passed down through the generations, heirlooms of sorts, like Grandpa's shotgun and Granny's Bible.

An Honorable Man

SEEING INTO THE FUTURE

TIMES WEREN'T BAD, BUT they weren't good either. It was somewhere in the middle and being squeezed from both ends. It was the place where the working class seems to always find itself, no matter who's in charge in Washington.

So around our house when I was growing up, an extra dollar was as big as a plow mule's behind and as scarce as a chainsaw with a conscience..

A mill worker like Daddy made enough wages to keep the smell of frying bacon in the kitchen, but not much extra. But I guess even that level of "get'n by" was still better than what he and Mama had left behind in south Alabama.

Outside of Enterprise, Alabama, around the time I was born, Daddy worked as a sharecropper. One season he and Mama scrimped, scraped and saved enough money to buy an electric refrigerator and get rid of the old icebox. It took a year, but they got the money saved. Their "needs" kept getting in the way of their "wants." But they were about to experience the future and it tasted like ice cream.

Back then, when you were church-mouse poor and smelled like a sweaty mule, buying on time was not an option. And you couldn't blame the storekeeper because he, like the farmer, just couldn't be sure when or if the rains would come.

But the future was coming, rain or no rain.

"Them thangs gonna put me out of bi'ness," said the ice delivery man after Daddy told him they would not need any more ice delivered. I guess the man could not only deliver ice but also see into the future. Daddy and the storekeeper should have asked him if it was going to rain or not.

But money has never been the yardstick to measure a man's worth. And Daddy was the prime example of that, as were many other mill-working men in the small town of Wewahitchka, Florida.

Those men, at least the ones I knew of, had one thing of value they prized above dollar bills—even if you couldn't pay the light bill with it—and that was their good name, their reputation.

It takes a lifetime to build a good name and only an eye blink to tear it down. By his actions, Daddy instructed me on ways to keep that good name up and standing once you got it built. One way was to always keep your word. "If you promise something, you better do everything within your power to keep that promise," Daddy said. "Or go explain why you can't."

Daddy's first promise was to himself, so I guess you can never be too young to learn that lesson.

"When I was a boy, not much bigger than you," he said, "I made a promise to myself that when I got grown, I'd never wear another pair of overalls."

He kept that promise. That told me a lot about the construction of his character early on. A boy who will keep a promise to himself will grow into a man who will keep a promise to you.

For many years, I witnessed him keeping his word to others.

During the early 1960s, he bought Mama a wringer washing machine with a handshake-backed promise to pay. You know the machine I'm talking about. The kind that would catch your fingers in the wringer like a snapping turtle with a "Maytag" logo stamped on his head. It would grab hold and leave you praying for thunder. Daddy probably got that machine from Mr. Claude Lister's store, probably without signing any paperwork, because when men like Woodrow Blackman shook your hand, there was no "probably" about it. As long as the mill whistle blew, you got your money.

To a good storekeeper back then, the feel of a man's hand said a lot about his character. And Daddy's hands were like so many other hands of working men, weathered from keeping promises. In Daddy's case, his were weathered more than most because no company made a pair of gloves that would fit his hands. His leathery hands were like other leathery hands in one way, but so unlike them in another. He had six fingers on each hand. Well, more precisely, five fingers and a thumb, all usable. Polydactyly is the name given to his extra pinkies. But honor was the name given to his handshake, no matter how many fingers were involved.

People used to kid him and say he could do higher math than the rest of them because of those extra digits. I always wished he'd taken up the guitar picking instead of the harmonica blowing. His uniqueness would have enabled him to make chords unreachable by the rest of us pickers. All we could have done would have been to stand around with our mouths open and whimper and whine, wishing we had been blessed with polydactyly.

By And By, Lord

KEEPING THE CIRCLE UNBROKEN

MOST PEOPLE KNEW MAMA by two names—Aunt Kat or Sister Blackman.

In "born again" circles, she was Sister Blackman, the helpmate to Brother Blackman, my daddy, whose thunder-and-lightning sermons could send sin scurrying out the door trying to get away from the storm.

He could do the same thing to church visitors from a quieter religion who were unaccustomed to such a deafening Disciple of Decibels. He could also send them double timing it out the door with one hand over an ear and the other hand holding a paper fan with a funeral home ad on it. It seems the funeral home was running a twofer sale on burial plots. "Die one and get one free," the ad read.

And a preacher said, "You 'bout as well run on out the doe and get yoself a can of stop leak and a mop cause God done punched a hole in yo sinful heart and the Devil is spill'n out all over the flo!"

And the people who remained inside the church said, "Amen."

One of those people was probably Sister Blackman. She was used to the noise.

In our family circle, including a small army of nieces and nephews around Wewahitchka, Florida, Mama was Aunt Kat.

This Florida batch of first cousins was begat mostly by two of Mama's sisters, Aunt Dot and Aunt Mazie. During the early 1950s, they followed their husbands, as Mama did hers, from south Alabama to North Florida. They were all searching for a new life that had nothing to do with black mules, hoe handles, and cotton patches. A third sister, Aunt Eunice and her husband also moved to Wewa. They never had children to add to the pot of pranksters.

Not to worry though. Aunt Mazie having 12 children and Aunt Dot having 3 made up for the shortfall.

My brother and I brought the total cousin-count to 17, which was a noticeable part of the population in that end of Gulf County.

That number doesn't even account for later on when the begets began to go forth and multiply. Then the begets of the begets began begetting, and the crowd grew.

But despite having all this family close by, Mama, for all of her life, still loved to visit her people in Alabama. That's what families did back then, they visited. Such closeness kept the family circle from coming off the rim and slinging apart like a high-mileage, recapped tire.

By Wednesday, she would have packed a few clothes in a brown paper IGA sack. Then, on Thursday, while holding my hand, we'd board a Greyhound bus that stopped once a week at the Gulf station in Wewahitchka.

From there, we'd be off on a five-hour trip to Dothan to see our northern people. I called them "our northern people" because to me, visiting kin in Dothan was as close to being around a northerner as I figured to get.

It was only a 70 mile trip, but a slow, slow go. Well, not really "go" in the sense of a direct path, but sort of zigging, zagging and drifting in a mostly northerly direction. "We'll get there by and by, Lord, by and by," Mama would say, reciting the words from an old gospel song about an unbroken circle.

The reason the trip took so long was because the bus also stopped to pick up and deliver bags of mail to several small outposts along the way. Plus, there was a bus change in Marianna.

When we finally got to Granny's house, Mama would go straight to a back bedroom and unpack our paper sack. After a day or so of the adults visiting and me and my cousin Donald staying in trouble, we'd complete the circle by repacking our sack and returning to Wewahitchka. Cousin Donald and I stayed in trouble because we liked to chase Grandpa's chickens until they wanted to lie down and rest instead of laying eggs.

The frequency of these circling trips to Dothan and back increased after Daddy got a decent car. It was a 1956 Chevy, two-tone with a "hood bird" ornament. Its left, bullet-shaped tail light, when twisted just right and lowered, doubled as the gas cap.

The route from Wewa to Dothan never varied much except for an occasional side trip to visit Daddy's people in Dale County near the Choctawhatchee River. That added a few more miles to the trip.

We got to the Blackman house by mid-morning, and by mid-afternoon, me and my cousin Bobby had already gotten into as much trouble with chickens as me and my Dothan cousin had.

With a Zebco rod and reel in hand, a rubber worm with the hook removed and the worm tied by monofilament, we walked to the chicken yard in search of that old rooster.

"There he is!" Bobby said as he spotted the rooster about the same time the rooster spotted us.

With the accuracy of a bass pro you might see on a fishing show, Bobby brought the rod back over his shoulder. Then, in one fluid motion, he brought it forward, released the button and the rubber worm dropped at the rooster's feet. Bobby would reel slowly, and the rooster and a few of the hens would start following their destiny. Like a snake in a greedy grab for a frog, the rooster snatched up the worm, clamped down and off he ran before the hens had a chance at it.

"IT'S MINE!" I'm sure he was saying in chicken chatter with part of the fake worm dangling out one side of his beak and the hens in pursuit to snatch it away, or try anyway. It didn't matter that it tasted more like a bike inner tube than a wiggler, it still looked like a worm.

The Zebco hummed and the drag clicked as the line zipped out.

And just think, before this fishing excursion, I thought a string tied to a June bug's leg was entertaining.

There was one point when I thought I could smell smoke coming from the reel. Maybe I didn't, but I sure thought I did,

Bobby slowly reeled in a round or two, the rod bending as the rooster took off again. Nobody was going to take that prize from him, especially two boys with red clay on their britches and watermelon on their breath.

After the rooster tuckered out, and before Uncle Howard or Aunt Lois caught us, Bobby gave the rod an upward snatch and the rubber worm popped out.

In my 10-year-old opinion, such adventures made the extra miles to Dale County well worth the gas and time.

But it really wasn't all that much extra time and effort. You can go far and do it fast when you have a decent car and no mail stops along the way.

This section of Dale County is where both sides of my family farmed. That is until government's eminent domain laws turned their red clay furrows into Fort Rucker's runways for future helicopter pilots too young to shave.

Forced out of the farming business, Mama's people, the Martins, ended up around Dothan. That's where the Florida people—that would be us—went to visit them with paper suitcases in hand.

Until early adulthood, this was as far north as I'd ever been, as far north as I ever wanted to be. So to me, if you were from anywhere north of Dothan, say Montgomery, you were a Yankee.

But that was alright. Looking back, I can see that we really didn't need to go any farther. Dothan and Dale County were far enough.

It's clear to me now how important it was then for my folks to go there.

It just made sense—a sense of place, a sense of belonging, a sense of purpose in keeping that family circle intact, to make their people my people. Then they could leave there and go back to Florida with their mission accomplished and their souls restored.

Even if getting there "by and by" meant long trips in a Greyhound with a paper bag suitcase on the floor by your seat, and later long trips in a '56 Chevy with a glass gas cap. These excursions to call on our northern kin were necessary if that circle was to remain unbroken, just like it said in Mama's old song... "Will the circle be unbroken. By and by, Lord, by and by."

Mule's In The Ditch

CAN TO CAN'T

Life looks different when you are viewing it with sweat in your eyes and sighting down one end of a taped-together hoe handle at your young beans wilting on the other end.

I am not about to tell you I have spent a lifetime, a week, or even a day attached to the end a hoe handle. I just haven't—wouldn't want to either. But my ancestors did, which means my genes know what a hoe handle feels like. I believe that is why hard work does not frighten me. It never has.

These are the very same sunburnt Martin genes that fueled my ability to play the guitar. The Blackman pool washed me down with a work ethic too, plus a deep desire and affection for holding babies. It's a tossup to me which smells better, a coconut cake or a baby's head. It's got to be a gift Blackman men are given at birth. They can take a plate piled with one ear of corn, two fried chicken breasts, scoops of beans and peas and fried okra, three biscuits and a slab of pound cake crowning it all. Then they can balance that plate on one knee while balancing and bouncing a baby on the other knee, and never drop either. That has got to be a gift a person inherits. If it's not, it ought to be.

A knack for gardening is also supposed to be in my genes, put there by both sides of the family. But, I guess in the rush of things in Alabama on the day I was born, fate got confused and put a cloth diaper on me instead of that pair of genes.

The green turnip-machine gene I never got. When it comes to producing anything using dirt, my talent turned out to be taking sweat mixed with grime and collecting it in the creased skin under my childhood neck. Mama called them "dirt beads," and they were the only jewelry the children of the working class could afford to wear, or the children of the holiness faith were allowed to wear.

But I love trying to grow things. I am envious of people who make gardening look as easy as riding a mule in the direction he wants to go. Some people can throw a handful of seed into the air and they will germinate and grow and rain squash from the heavens.

I have farming experience, though. Daddy, a plow-hand from way back, one time rigged up a single tree on the front of his push plow, tied a rope around my waist and hooked me to the plow.

"Step up, Bill," he said in a Sunday school rendition of his watered-down mule tone. Then he clucked and drove me like a young, skinny mule missing two legs and his two long ears. I guess that goes to show you that old habits are hard to break. Other than me giving out before I got to the end of a short row and Daddy giving up on me before then as a mule fill-in, the only problem I had was getting my "gee" and my "haw" confused. This Muleology with its lingo was new to me, but as second nature to him as coughing up that old paper mill smoke.

Many of my kinfolks got that tillage talent. They are such excellent gardeners that when they walk down a furrow dropping corn seed, the iron skillets hanging on the kitchen wall will break out in a sweat in anticipation of doing their part to make Sunday dinner a double blessings affair. That's what I was told, anyway.

Whether it was farming or pulpwooding, logging or sawmill work, my ancestors labored hard and seemed to thrive and stay alive on it, as if it tasted like hot cornbread and rejuvenated like a glass of cold buttermilk. I'm sure they didn't know for sure if life had them in a headlock or was just hugging them extra hard, but it didn't matter. Hard work and sweat would be the legacy they passed on to their children, just like playing music, preaching the gospel, and crooning babies.

Though they worked as hard as they did, toiling from dark to dark, six days a week, they did not work on that seventh day. That day had been set aside long before they came along as the "Day Of Rest."

At least they tried not to work on that day.

This "No Work On The Lord's Day" rule was only a guideline, not a law.

The reason it was only a guideline was because mules never put much thought to the rules of religion. The only rule a mule had then, or now, is that no rules exist for mules. That's probably why they are not mentioned in the 10 Commandments

"Sometimes your mule and wagon is in the ditch and you gotta get him out no matter what day it ist," Mama would say when asked about how rigid this "no work on Sunday" policy was.

That's also what she'd say when I had to play music on a Sunday somewhere other than church. "Well, I guess your wagon is in the ditch today," she'd say.

Other than for the womenfolk—who still had just as many plates to fill on Sunday as on any other day—it was easy to live by this rule. That is, until that crazy mule drags your wagon into the ditch on your way home from church. I guess since God created the mule... well, really, the mule is man-made—a cross between a horse and a donkey, so I'll rephrase that. Since God gave man the nod to go ahead with that union, He knew He'd also need to create a Sunday work exemption to go along with the mule. If the truth be known, He created a mule communication exemption for the same reason, which gave you one more thing to ask forgiveness for come Sunday.

Though that Sunday work law was bendable, Mama was strict when it came to the Lord and His other rules and their enforcement. She thought a fast draw and good aim with a stout switch was just as effective as memorizing Bible verses. Probably more so! I don't know if it was because she aimed where she hit or hit where she aimed. All I know is she seldom missed.

I believe this tendency to "switch first and ask questions later" was genetic in her. To hear her talk about it, Grandpa Martin, her daddy, was pretty fast on the draw, too.

"He didn't do it out of meanness," she said. "But when you needed it, he'd whip you in a hurry with whatever was handy."

The problem with wearing overalls is that you don't need a belt, and it's hard to discipline a child with a gallus. So Grandpa Martin grabbed whatever would work and was within reach. I don't think Granny Martin was that way. But when pushed, her ability to pick a good switch was proven to me and my cousin Donald once after we picked a green peach from her tree.

But when your genes wear overalls raveled around the edges from generations of hard work, you soon lose your fear of switches. In fact, you don't fear much of anything, except maybe getting too old to work anymore, not being much good for anything to anybody anymore. You fear a lack of busyness where every day becomes a forced day of rest. And you fear that more than you fear death itself.

But, you can always grow yourself a garden, or try. That will give you something to do. Or better yet, buy yourself a plow mule. That'll have you seeking Sundays again, if not for a day off from work, then to ask for forgiveness because of your colorful language.

That Polident Glow

PUCKS AND PREACHERS

DADDY WASN'T IN TROUBLE with the law, but he and his soul were in trouble with the Lord—that is, if you listened to Mama.

I've seen old pictures of him where his outside shell looked damaged. He was not born that way. Life made him that way. It's hard to keep your outside spit shined when your life is filled with hard dirt and hard-headed mules, pockets of IOUs and dead-end cotton rows that were just another place to turn his plow around and start over again.

But if you looked close, past the outside, the inside was alright.

"He was a good man," Mama said.

"But I can promise you that good men don't always get to walk through them pearly gates," she said. "Being good is not enough. Your Daddy's soul was in trouble and he needed to find Jesus if he wants to get in."

Daddy did find Jesus, not along the Biblical shores of Galilee, but under a used circus tent pitched on the baseball field in Port St. Joe, Florida, on a summer night around 1958.

The tent belonged to Evangelist T. L. Lowery. Every night for a week Brother Lowery was inside, sweat'n and shout'n and pitch'n Jesus and using no curveballs, just straight and fast, right over Heaven's home plate.

Then one afternoon after a smelly day at the paper mill, Daddy washed and put on his "town" shoes. He loaded us into the car and drove the 24 miles to that tent. Under that canvas, God washed him again. This time not in soapy water but in the "Blood of the Lamb." I sat on a folding chair and watched wide-eyed.

Brother Newsome, a paper mill co-worker and part-time preacher from White City, had talked Daddy into meeting him at the tent revival that night.

I guess God and Brother Newsome teamed up to recruit potential new talent who could keep their eye on the ball and hit a home run for Jesus ever now and then.

Some preachers can launch scriptures that leave a smoke trail behind each Holy Roller missile. Brother Newsome had that ability, and the willingness to launch. These "Roller" rockets got their launch code straight from the Bible, sometimes from Deuteronomy, sometimes from another fueling source, such as Leviticus.

To go along with that ability was his inability to keep his false teeth where they were supposed to be.

Sometimes when his sermon reached a fiery mountain top, not only would he launch scriptural missiles that had sinners on the back row ducking and squirming, but sometimes he'd also thrust forth his false teeth.

Through the years I remember more than once hearing his uppers click against his lowers as the countdown to launch neared.

Then they'd bulge out a little, and he'd push them back in. Then they'd rattle again in what sounded a lot like the second verse of "I'll Fly Away."

A few hallelujahs later, they'd do it again, peeping out as if trying to muster the courage to jump. After all, he was tall, and it was a long way to the floor.

Then in a well-timed convulsion, between the "halle" and the "lujah", they would go forth, the uppers and lowers, scooting across the planked church floor like spirit-filled hockey pucks with a Polident glow.

Once they stopped, he would track their path as people began lifting their feet off the floor. After he caught up with them, he'd reach and grab them as if he were a goalie in a sweaty white shirt and thin black necktie. Then he'd pick them up, shout a few more times, dance in place, then stick them in his pocket.

"And the Lawd said," he'd shout while he danced in place, "don't let nothing corrupt come out yo mouth." Then he'd dance a few more steps. "I hope He weren't talking 'bout false teeth."

That was a bona fide, pass-the-offering-plate crowd pleaser.

Believe me, you can not say that you have ever been fully sermonized to a point where you are hunting the door or hunting the altar until you've had a set of uppers and lowers filled with the holy spirit bounce across the floor and scoot in your general direction with a shout'n preacher chasing after them.

That sight was enough to get any self-sanctifying sinner to a point between soul searching and laughing.

And Brother Newsome preached, "Don't you look down your stiff religious nose at me when you know that by the end of this night, you'll be the one dancin' on top of that pew and holding a hymnal over yo head!"

After we got home that night after leaving Lowery's tent, and with foul-line chalk on his knees, Daddy said his entire world changed. Everything was now in place; everything was now at peace.

Later he would tell folks, "When I got home that night, even the dog and cat were eatin' out of the same pan," he said. "The dog was a'preach'n, and the cat was a'shout'n," he said with a hint of holiness on his breath.

That ball field that night was my first memory of a holiness encounter. I guess I was about seven years old. I don't remember being in a church before that—plenty of times after that.

All I remember was the noise, the excitement, men and women full of the holy spirit and dancing around like Elvis impersonators. It was some show.

I guess one of Brother Lowery's prophetic fast balls hit Daddy, because the next thing I saw was him being led to the front by Brother Newsome. Both men were crying. Daddy looked like he was walking on water. But it might have just been those "town" shoes hurting his feet.

That was the first time I remember seeing Daddy cry. I guess that's one reason I remember that night. This genuine man of God influenced my life from that point on. Not so much with words, but with actions. God's faithful servants, like Daddy, preached their sermons as much with their lives as with their lips. Later, I also gained a moral profit from being hauled by this prophet to and from dirt-road revival meetings where he preached.

Religion is like a flashlight. If you want to keep it shining, you have to recharge the batteries.

I guess Daddy saw those revival meetings he preached—strung out in little churches from East Point, Florida, to Cottonwood, Alabama—as a way he could help folks recharge their religious batteries and keep their godly light shining.

And the children sang, "This little light of mine, I'm gonna let it shine. Let it shine, let it shine, let it shine."

Lord help, where would I have ended up without that influence to guide me, without his lot of Bible and his little bit of belt?

But Daddy's goodness has always been a bright light, even long before he became the "polydactyl preacher."

I have an older cousin who remembers 1950 and '51. She told me about south Alabama and the dark times Mama and Daddy went through, not only physically but emotionally.

Sharecropping has never been known for producing much cotton or cash. So Mama probably didn't go to the doctor when she was pregnant. A doctor could have helped.

"You're lucky to be alive," my cousin Mary told me. "Your Mama had a rough time getting you into this world."

But she got me here, and she and Daddy kept me here—she and Daddy and some doctor at the hospital in Enterprise, Alabama.

With nothing in his pocket but promises, I don't know how Daddy ever got that doctor paid.

But I guarantee you he did! Because he was a good man even before he met Jesus, just like Mama said.

The Loud Bunch

EARS RING'N AND BUTT STING'N

THOUGH WE DIDN'T TALK much, I do remember a lot of things Daddy told me when I was little. Sometimes we'd walk for miles without either of us saying much. Our lack of words wasn't because we didn't like each other, but simply because he was a quiet man raising a son who took after him.

He suffered a lot during his last days here on this earth, bad days made bearable by the good/evil drugs—your opinion depending on your pain level. We didn't talk much during those days either, because I was here and he was there. I could have been there more. I should have been there more.

Just after he got the long face from the doctor, and before the cancer dug in its heels and began its dirty work, I remember him talking about a "To Do" list when he got to Heaven.

He knew exactly what was #1 on that list.

"I already know the first thang I'm gonna do when I cross that pearly threshold," he said with his eyes tilted upward toward Home and his twelve-fingers reaching for the sky, "I'm gonna go find my mama."

A few years later, I believe he did just that as my brother and I stood at the foot of his bed while Mama's tears dampened Daddy's chest. That was October 15, 2003. That's when he drew his last breaths while lying in his bed inside the first and only house he and Mama ever owned.

Then, between breaths that got farther and farther apart, he was gone… gone to find his mama.

Daddy's death was quiet, just as his life was quiet. Quiet, that is, unless he was chunking scriptures at you from behind, in front of, and sometimes on top of a trembling pine altar. From there, he was about as quiet as a loaded pulpwood truck missing a muffler and pulling out of a bog.

No, he wasn't much of a talker. But he was a shouting preacher who could scare the devil right out of you, no matter how tight a chokehold Satan had on your heart. When "the Spirit" grabbed hold of Daddy, he became a true apostle of colossal.

As a child, I left the church more than once with my ears ringing and my butt stinging. My ears ringing from that Disciple of Decibels, that preacher man with polydactyly—the Reverend Woodrow Blackman. My butt was stinging from a mama who had no tolerance for boyish nose-pickers with their pranks and snickers. So after warning you once about how lightning strikes boys who misbehave in church, it didn't bother her one bit to give you a good reason to pray that a lightning bolt would swoop down and strike you just to give you some relief from the wrath of a preacher's wife.

Throughout North Florida and south Alabama, Daddy became poetically known as "That preacher man with six fingers on each hand. That preacher man who laughed and shouted, but no one ever doubted. That preacher man who once plowed sod but is now a true man of God."

Unless they took the time to count, most people noticed nothing different about his hands. That is unless you happen to be a glove salesman.

That extra pinky on each hand never got in his way until he needed to wear gloves. The rarity of six-finger gloves at the hardware store is why his hands were so callused. But those hard hands were in wonderful contrast to his soft heart.

He was even-tempered and tolerant. I never saw him lose his temper, not even while he was trying to whip his first set of dentures. "It takes a man to whip a set of false teeth," he was fond of saying after the fight was over and he came out the victor. I guess he figured if Granny Martin, his sparrow-like mother-in-law in Alabama, could do it, then he could, too.

Though he never said it, I think his motto might have been, "You don't rid yourself of a really bad temper by losing it." He came close after his encounter with a mule named Rodie. But that's a story for later on.

I'm ashamed to say I don't have a photo of Daddy's hands. Judging from photos I have of him as a child, he must have been ashamed of his hands because when the camera came out, his hands went in his pockets. Either that or he curled his fingers backwards, hiding them from the shutter.

And later on after his hands became his calling card, I just never thought about taking any pictures that included his hands. Like a lot of things in life, it just wasn't as important then as it is now. It didn't matter then like it matters now.

But I guess if you think about it, his hands were not what made him unique as most men go. The secret wasn't the hand. The secret was the man. And I do have photos of the man—pictures in a box, in my mind, and in my blood.

Daddy was an ordained Assembly of God minister. Both the men and women of that faith were a loud bunch, sometimes to the point of sometimes, when they got real happy, making your ears ring. Especially after the pulpit got amplified.

To be honest with you, as a boy I was never afraid of the holiness women in their long dresses, long sleeves and long hair—women who hugged your neck, shouted praises to God, spoke in tongues, pinched your cheeks and smelled like a full Avon sample case. I ought to have been afraid of them, but I just wasn't. I was used to them.

I'm sure that to some passerby naïve to the sights and sounds of such noisy religions, some curious sinner drawn to the church window by escaping decibels, he or she would find it unnerving to see little children quietly seated amongst all them "holy rollers" unraveling on the other side of that glass.

For those who do not know, "holy rollers" are not the patched tires on the preacher's Chevy, but Southern slang for the shout'n people of the holiness religion. I guess they were called "holy rollers" because sometimes they'd get real happy and roll around on the floor.

To me as a young'un, it was all as much a part of my life as Black Diamond guitar strings and dreams of getting paid to play my guitar. Every Wednesday night and most of the day on Sundays, if those church doors were open, Daddy was going to be there. And, since Mama was going with him, that meant me and my brother, too.

Through experience and exposure, it got to where I could tell what the night was going to be like just by the song service.

The choir was made up of volunteers from the congregation who walked up front after being summoned by the preacher. "Y'all come on up here and let's make a joyful noise unto the Lord," he'd say. Then I'd hear the pews and knees crackle as people pulled themselves up to amble up front. Once there, they'd turn around to face the shyer ones who were left behind to listen and clap like cheerleaders each time God scored a point against the Devil.

Most of the time, the choir sang only a few songs, and it was over. Then the service went on to the next step where the preacher read off a list of names, mostly prayer requests for the "sick and shut-ins," those being people confined to bed and unable to come to church.

But sometimes, somewhere about the fourth verse of "I Shall Not Be Moved," somebody, somewhere would throw a switch and send a charge of energy into the proceedings. That's when people started shuddering and shaking like the preacher had pulled out a sack of snakes. And as the volume went up, so too did the energy level.

The men, who smelled like Old Spice and paper mill smoke, and the women, who smelled like Juicy Fruit gum and Skin So Soft, began to stomp their feet and dance around. It was like fiery brimstone had fallen from the preacher's sermon notes and landed inside their shoes.

If you've never been to a full-throttled holiness meeting, I tell you it can look a little like a bar brawl, just minus the whiskey, the fists and the police involvement.

Daddy would be right in the middle of them, whooping and hollering and waving his six-fingered hands in the air.

On the occasions when Daddy was the preacher at a church, polydactyly gave him an advantage over other preachers. That extra finger enabled him to use one hand and point at six different sinners at once—twelve if he used both hands. God gave him six-shooters, and he was not afraid to draw them. That's unlike your run-of-the-mill preachers who can only point at five—ten at the most—sinners who needed to be "washed in the blood." But Daddy did have to be careful when anointing someone's forehead with olive oil to pray for them. He might poke them in the eye with that dangling polydactyl pinky.

But when he was part of the congregation and not the preacher, Daddy would make a joyful noise along with the rest of them, because he still could. At that point, the paper mill had yet to take his breath away.

And the women would shake their heads until the bobby pins shook loose and began to fly around like metallic skeeter hawks. It was an unraveling of sorts that allowed their now liberated hair to fall to their waistlines as the bobby pins hit the floor. But that was okay because a new card of bobby-pins only cost a dime.

Then somebody would begin to "speak in tongues," and in an instant it would get as quiet as a cat leaving a room, all waiting for the interpreter to speak. But the quietness was only a damp spot in the fuse, because after the interpreter spoke, the spirit would explode again with even more bang than before.

I never could figure out who it was that threw that switch and sent that electric charge into the crowd. The preacher blamed it on God. Thinking back, I think he was right.

At the time, though, I never knew who did it. But what I did know was that on those nights, it would be 11 o'clock before I'd get in bed, and it was a school night too. So I learned to catch a quick nap while everyone else was running around inside the church and sometimes outside. And Mama didn't seem to mind if I did. If she did, she never pinched me.

And the preacher said, "I know y'all thinking 'bout that left-over fried chicken at home. But just give me a few mo minutes and I'll be like Pharaoh and let God's people go. Can I get a amen?"

Since I haven't traveled much, I can only guess that such churches were a Southern thing, kind of like cornbread and iron skillets, or corn whiskey and copper kettles.

But Southern or not, it was more than a Sunday and Wednesday routine, more than a guaranteed seat on the bus to the Promise Land. It was part of Southern culture, my parents' culture, my culture. And it is getting as scarce as dime packs of bobby-pins and preachers who can point at six sinners with one hand tied behind his back.

Miracles

THE SANTA I WILL NEVER FORGET

Even in pictures, Daddy had a sharp stare that seemed to telegraph that he meant business, like he was barking out orders to a mule.

Woodrow Blackman seemed to look right through you to the point where you wanted to turn around and look behind you just to see who or what he was looking at.

It was a look that made you think he just might have been toting a cheap pistol in the bib pocket of his overalls, when really all that was in there was his harmonica.

His hat tilted down to the left and his smile and eyebrow tilted up to meet it, as if they were holding it up.

He looked like he had it all figured out as he stood in front of that painted board in Enterprise, Alabama, to have his picture made in a new hat, his Sunday overalls and borrowed black coat.

It was almost as if he was saying, "Come on life. I dare you!"

He looked like someone who believed—if in nothing else—in himself. He looked as if he'd won.

But if you have little to lose, then it's easy to win. And he had little to lose back then.

That's what growing up hard will do to you—give you corn-confidence even if you're on a pig-weed budget and you had to borrow a black coat to get your picture made.

By the time I came along, the mules and long days in the sun had robbed him of his spunk. He still had that piercing stare. It just didn't go as deep as it once had.

The first memory of Daddy I have is in Wewahitchka, Florida, inside that airy house he and Mama borrowed month-to-month from Mr. Mossy Cleckley.

It was Christmas morning, and I was too young to worry about showing up on Santa's "naughty" list because, up to that point, my biggest sin was peeing on an ant bed. For Christmas, Daddy and Mama had bought me a miniature metal Standard Oil service station. It came with little cars, rubber customers and rubber station attendants to wait on those rubber customers. I found everything under the tree except for the station attendants.

"I betcha Santa dropped 'em on his way back up the chimney," Daddy said. "Let's go see."

Taking my hand in his, we walked to the bedroom where the cold fireplace was. And guess what we found! A bag of plastic gas station attendants.

"There they are, on the floor in front of the chimney," Daddy said as he released my hand so he could point toward the little plastic bag full of rubber men. I ran over and grabbed them.

"Santa must'a been daydreaming and dropped them on his way back up the chimney after he got those presents out from under the bed to take to the little boy down the road," I said.

Mama had told me the toys I'd found under her bed a few days before Christmas belonged to that other boy.

Wearing her best poker face, she said, "Santa hid them there and he will pick them up on Christmas Eve to take to that boy's house."

"That was one lucky boy," I thought. "We are a lot alike, too, because he asked for the same things that I did."

I've thought about that morning a lot over the years. That was a special effort they went through just so I might believe in something unseen for a little while longer. Little did they know that would one day become Daddy's life calling to compel people to have faith enough to believe in something they couldn't see.

But that's not the only thing I remember about that Christmas.

The night before, Daddy and Mama had talked "Santa" into paying us a visit.

Up to that point, the closest I'd ever been to Santa was when he passed by riding on top of the firetruck, throwing out "jawbreakers" and peppermint during the Christmas parade in downtown Wewa.

And now I was about to meet him, and I didn't even know it. Decades later and that encounter is as fresh in my mind as it was the morning after it happened.

To be honest with you, it turns out Santa wasn't even a man. He was my Aunt Eunice, Mama's sister, dressed up in a Santa outfit. Where she borrowed a Santa suit in a small Florida Panhandle town during the 1950s, I'll never know. She might have made it herself from feed sacks. I didn't look, but "Purina Scratch Feed" might have been stamped across the seat of her pants. She even wore a cotton beard made from the entrails of an old pillow. From the sound of her clopping across the living room floor, she must have been wearing Uncle Roy's work boots.

Thinking back, I wonder if she had her black medicine bottle of doctor-prescribed "nervous medicine" in her pocket that night. I could have used a taste of it myself before the night was over—that is, if I hadn't been a child. But, like the truth about Santa and bottles of nerve medicine, some things you just need to keep out of the reach of children.

I was sitting with Mama on the couch in the living room, a picture of dogs playing poker hung on the wall behind us. Without even knocking, Santa barged through the front door. The sudden intrusion didn't startle Mama at all. It was almost as if she knew it was coming. I remember Santa bouncing in, holding up her britches with one hand. Her other hand was choking a sweat-stained pillowcase full of dime store treasures. It was a grab-and-go toy sack of sorts. She had no doubt snatched it from the bed in afterthought on her way out the door. The cap she wore was wrapped in what looked like the bloody-colored fur from a rabbit that had tried to cross the road and was runover by reindeer. It had a fluffy white tail dangling to one side, it being the only part left unstained. She jollied over to the couch and flopped down next to me. "Come over here and sit on my knee," she said with the air whistling between her missing teeth.

I remember trying to climb the back of that couch to get away, but found out quick that it's hard to get a toehold on that slick Naugahyde when your feet are sweating. I'm sure I looked like a panicking rat trying to climb up the inside wall of an empty lard bucket. There was a lot of action, but little progress. The couch's back was just too slick and steep. Aunt Eunice pulled off her hat and pulled the beard below her chin so maybe if I saw it was her, it would dilute my panic. But it made it worse. I don't know why it would have, unless I thought Santa had eaten poor old Aunt Eunice. That must have been it!

It was more of a Halloween event than a Christmas one. But it could have been worse. She could have had Uncle Roy with her. I could picture him dressed in a pair of red long Johns, the closest thing he had to an elf outfit. He would have had a bell on his hat, cotton balls taped to the toes of his brogans, and a "Prince Albert" can stuffed down his right candy-cane print sock where he could get to it if the urge struck. He would have been a self-made elf with a self-made cigarette dangling from the corner of his mouth and smoke drifting up past his frayed hair. I bet I could have clawed up the back of that couch then.

I guess that was just one more example of Mama and Daddy going out of their way to make me believe in Santa. Even to the point of Mama conspiring with her sister.

But looking back, I can understand why they wanted me to believe in Santa and the miracle of Christmas.

Only a few years earlier we were living in a planked shanty in Coffee County, Alabama, where Daddy was farming on halves and Mama was boiling "Pet" milk for a new baby.

The way they told it, we had enough to eat in 1951, but that was about it. There were no extras, no matter how hard Daddy worked that old mule. The future looked about as bright as the bottom of an empty wash pot.

And here we were now, five years later, a hundred miles south of there. Daddy had steady work at the paper mill where paychecks didn't hinge on the finickiness of the weather and a brain-dead beast. Mama was baking pies for the church's building fund and conspiring with Santa Claus. And we were living in a sturdy rental house with inside plumbing and a roof that didn't leak all that much.

So, to them, miracles did happen. How else could they explain their good fortune?

God Always Showed Up

THE WEWA WIGGLE

DOES ANYONE GIVE A damn anymore about ordinary hardworking folk who made up—and still make up—the backbone of this country? These are honest folks who cough a little, get high on Jesus, and sing about brighter days to come. These are the characters who would clasp calloused hands to clinch a deal. But like an old man trying to remember his way home, the memories of lives like these will soon disappear. Their embodiment will have crossed Jordan and gone home before we even realized their feet were wet.

Sure, some of these characters were rough and had a few splinters around the edges. Yes, their hands were dirty, but their hearts were clean, and they had more spunk than a case of kittens.

These are the kinds of people I grew up around, and I wonder if I have the right to prostitute their memory just so I can write words on a piece of paper. As a group, they deserve more than that. Much more!

Because of them, I will always be who I am: that "ol' boy" who grew up in Wewahitchka, Florida. That fact will never change. Like my hometown friend Tony Whitfield once said as we stood on a stage playing music and watching an old classmate of ours wiggle across the dance floor, "You can take the person outta Wewa," Tony said. "But you can't take the Wewa outta the person." I guess he was describing me, too.

By the way, that dance has a name, at least it did back home at the Cherokee Tavern. The "Wewa Wiggle." There is a song that goes along with it, too. The song is remembered by old tonkers who have not yet gone on, but who are getting close enough to the edge of the stage to get a little nervous. It's called "The Wewa Boogie" and is a relic of a song that is in danger of being misplaced behind a fading memory, or worse yet, lost under a coffin lid.

I didn't notice at the time, but childhood characters were as thick around me as summer gnats around a mushy watermelon.

One of those characters was an old, soft-spoken man who lived next to us for a while. He never wore shoes, no matter how frozen the ground. And year round, even in August, he wore overalls, a thick denim coat, a long-sleeve shirt buttoned up to his chin, and a black felt hat that made his white handlebar mustache shine like the reputation of a preacher's widow or the hood ornament on a '56 Chevy.

Sometimes I would see him sitting in his yard in a straight chair. He would be staring into distant tree tops as if he could see something I couldn't, keeping his thoughts quiet and confined under that black hat like memories lost in a dark cave. Then he'd look at the ground and sigh. Maybe he was about to doze. Or maybe he was just listening for an old echo from inside that hat.

It never occurred to me to ask what he was looking at. Now I wish I had talked to him more, much more. I never knew his last name, only his first and middle, Barefoot Charlie. I called him "Mr. Charlie" because, after all, respect for elders, like washing behind your ears, was a requirement when being raised in a preacher's household!

Mr. Charlie wasn't the only one. Another ancient soul would show up at our house on most Sundays. He always seemed to know when we got home from church. I don't think he had any supernatural powers, just following his nose.

Mama would always invite him in to join us at the Sunday table. The old man never turned her down or bowed his head when Daddy said the blessing. I know because I had one eye open, watching him watch the plate of fried chicken. He was already taking aim, his arm-spring wound tight and waiting to make its move.

The "Amen" would not have reached the ceiling before—as fast as a snake snatching a biddy—the drumstick would be gone.

Then within five minutes after wiping his mouth on his shirt sleeve, Mossy Cleckley would be on the front porch floor, sprawled on his side, snoring while a Sears catalog held up his head. Later, I wondered if insomnia ever tormented him after Sears discontinued their mail-out "paper pillows," the thick ones that included the Christmas toys. I never asked Mr. Mossy that question. I wish I had.

Then there were all those preachers when I was growing up. It was an Ark full of "Disciplined Disciples of Decibels" who threw scriptures at sinners like they were skipping rocks across the Jordan, all while exposing the Devil as a cross-dresser.

"HE CAN WEAR OVERALLS OUT IN THE FIELD. OR HE CAN WEAR SUITS WITH WORLDLY APPEAL. BUT I TELL YOU THE DEVIL IS HERE AND I TELL YOU THE DEVIL IS REAL... REAL... REAL," the preacher shouted as the people clapped their hands and danced in place.

They were full-throttled Bible-thumpers with an elevated respiration and heart palpitations. They wore shirts soaked in perspiration from preaching to a world caught up in desperation. And most of them smelled like "Old Spice."

Daddy was one of them. Once he "answered the call" to be the preacher of a church in Kinard, Florida. Most times, the only non-family member to show up to "hear the word" was a neighbor who nodded while sitting on the second pew from the front. Good thing he didn't bring a Sears catalog with him. If he had, he would've been sprawled on his side, snoring and dreaming about the fried chicken waiting on him back home. Hymnals just weren't thick enough to make good pillows.

I could have counted the biggest crowd that ever showed up with one hand tied behind my back. But God always showed up... always!

Daddy preached some of his best sermons to that one nodding man.

I consider myself blessed to have been around characters like these.

But when you're getting old, remembering can be treacherous. It can be like looking for the light switch in a dark room. You're apt to stub your toe on a chair leg, or step on a sleeping cat minding its own business, or stumble across some memory that you didn't realize you'd lost.

Dusty memories of many dirt road churches bounce around in my head, making noises like drink bottles on the floorboard of a Chevy bumping along a washboard road.

Those memories have a smell to them, too.

It's an aromatic combination of Juicy Fruit gum, Old Spice, Skin So Soft and fried chicken that filled the small cinder block church. Some called it the smell of "Pentecostal Potpourri." Others called it the "Holy Roller Roll-On."

Me, well... I called it wonderful. I still call it unforgettable.

I've always liked the intimacy of a small church as opposed to a large one. Inside those snug churches, rumors could get started because closeness had it where you could smell your pew neighbor's breath without even trying. "Ol Brother So-and-So's breath smelt like Listerine this morning," one sister would whisper to the other. "You know what that means," said the other. "Uh-huh," said the first.

I've attended big churches before, and the people were friendly enough. But I just didn't sense the same closeness when the church was so big that the preacher didn't even know your name. But, on the plus side, he didn't know your reputation either.

It could also be because in a big church there is too much space between the front pew and the pulpit. I think preachers need to be close enough to the flock to nod a nose-bumping howdy to the almost nodding parishioner. Minds can drift to lonely fishing holes when there's too much space between the howdies and the hallelujahs. I know. I've nodded there before.

In the small church the preacher is so close to the front pew that if he gets overly happy, his false teeth might just land in old Sister So-and-So's lap. That's all it would take to start a chain reaction of shouting, foot stomping and hand fans flying through the air like birds made of wood and paper, all with "Independent Life Insurance Company" stamped on their wings.

Daddy traveled and preached in many back road churches like these—cinder block tabernacles that stretched out across North Florida and south Alabama. They were temples of God daubed with a history of calluses and galluses, okra stings and gospel sings.

As a young adult and recovering sinner, I liked to attend those same types of churches. I was there to hedge my bet against falling into that "Lake Of Fire" the preachers liked to refer to as my "fiery finale to the Honky Tonk Tour"—or worse than falling into the lake, being pushed in.

But as a child, I had no choice but to be dragged along on Daddy's "Foot Washers" tour. I'm glad now he made me go.

No padded pews in those churches—the plank seats as hard and unbending as the working class folks who sat on them. When the people stood to pray, the pew seats and the peoples' backs creaked in harmony, as if the choir director was leading them in a familiar gospel favorite.

Me, I could almost hear Haggard singing "I'll drink a little beer in a tavern, sing a little bit of these working man blues." I'm pretty sure some of the men might have frolicked a little too hard the night before and were recovering from more than pew buns and sore backs. And now, at their wife's urging because they hated the sin but loved the sinner, they found themselves stuck in God's House somewhere between recovery and Calvary.

The way I figured it, they had slipped into the ditch and were there to ask God to pull them out... again. I figured God has plenty of tow-chains and was glad to do it. He knew they were just trying to cushion their existence from a lifetime of stoop labor, and He knew that if anybody deserved an occasional do-si-do, these folks did. Besides, sometimes you need a little sip if you want to sound believable when you tell the bathroom mirror every morning that things will get better one day.

I'm no Bible scholar, but I bet the Road to Calvary has a few watering holes along the way.

But when you figured the sum of the parts, this was an honest bunch. They were men in overalls and women in long-sleeved, long-bottomed dresses that started early (up around their necks) and ended late (down around their ankles).

These were a class of folks that were easy to spot since the hinges on their eye glasses were taped together. New eyeglasses were way down on the list by the time the first of the month rolled around. These same people had the spines on their worn Bibles patched with that same tape. A new Bible would mean having to re-underline all those favorite passages. And there were decades of them.

Yep, they were an excellent class of folks. Their hands might have needed a scrubbing, but their hearts had been "Washed in the Blood."

It didn't matter to me then—and it doesn't now—if sometimes they got a little sideways in the ditch with the "Thou shalt nots."

I can relate. My farrier business has me driving the back Georgia roads between Recovery—near the Flint River and Calvary—along GA 111. Some of the back roads are the color of dusty blood, and sometimes, after a good rain, the consistency of a tomato milk shake.

My past job as a musician had me traveling those same roads after dark. So, I know now—and I knew then—what it's like to live with the possibility of getting sideways in the ditch and ending up stuck somewhere between Recovery and Calvary.

Fly Flaps and Shout'n Preachers

ARMED AND DANGEROUS

Grandpa Martin's hair was as white as a holiness preacher's shirt before he gets wound up and happy. As far back as I can remember, his hair had always been that white.

He'd sit on their small porch on the hot days when the air was too thin to sop and too syrupy to wear. There, in a straight chair under the shade of a tin roof that popped as the hot sun pulled on the nails, he'd spend the heat of the day killing houseflies with a homemade fly flap constructed by his wife, Maude Bell (Marchman) Martin.

If he was as thrifty as some of his children claimed, he probably wouldn't allow Granny Martin to buy a new fly flap. "Ah, he's so stingy he can sit on a penny and tell you if it's heads or tails," they'd say. "Bless his heart."

When doing battle with flies, Grandpa's weapon of choice was fashioned from a folded-over piece of window screen with cloth sewn around the edges to hold it together. Granny did the sewing. She also attached a double-twisted coat hanger long enough so Grandpa only had to lean out from his chair a little to deliver his deadly intent. The flies never knew what hit them.

Flies are hard to catch napping. But despite their alertness, he didn't miss many. By afternoon the proof of his accuracy lay in small piles on the ground, making the red Alabama dirt look like a new orange ice cream flavor with winged Oreos crumbled on top. The topping was motionless, except for the ones the ants were dragging back home with them. Ants have families to feed, too.

If flies had the ability to hang onto a little hammer, they would have nailed up wanted posters on every tree, each poster having Grandpa's picture plastered on it. "ARMED AND DANGEROUS—Robert Lee Martin, aka 'Stay Off My Porch' Martin. For the crime of Housefly Genocide. Approach With Caution."

This quiet little man wearing suspenders and sneaking up on flies with a homemade fly flap was my mama's daddy, my grandfather.

My first memory of him was not at this house where he sat and flapped flies and spit snuff into a coffee can, but another porch only a mile away, but still along Lingo Road outside Dothan, Alabama.

I remember the outside of that house had tar-paper siding that was made to look like brick. Thinking back, I guess fake brick was like a gritty makeup people used to cover the truth that the inhabitants were closer to living in poverty than they were to living in a brick house. Dangling from the front, like an afterthought when you have a few boards left over, was a porch adorned with a couple of straight chairs with cowhide bottoms.

Later on, he and Granny moved to where he sat on the porch that I remember best, guarding the door to the house with a fly flap and passing time by sending houseflies to meet their maker.

That little house is where we visited a lot when I was growing up.

Mama's brother, Tommy Martin, lived next door. Like Daddy, Uncle Tommy was also a holiness preacher. He and his family attended Brother Lloyd Snelgrove's church in Midland City. Daddy loved to go to that church and attended most every time we visited Mama's people.

During that time, Uncle Tommy also had a weekly radio show. But there was nothing "weakly" about it. There he and others shook the walls as he preached and they shouted; he played guitar and they sang at varying volume between commercials, spreading a joyful noise out to all the lost souls strung out across radio-land.

"God don't need to smell yo breath to know that last night you were a'boot'n and scoot'n and a'back slide'n," came the staticky voice across the radio. Uncle Tommy could speak with authority on juke joints because he played the tonk tour before finely tuning his guitar to the key of "J" for "Jesus."

Sometimes when we were visiting, Daddy—who had played his harmonica in a few dance halls—would preach on the radio too.

I bet with the wattage those two put out, you would have been hard pressed to find the Devil hanging out around the parking lot, looking for a straggling sinner.

That was back when Southern preachers pounded podiums and were not ashamed or afraid to tell the Devil to go to hell. And they did it with the delivery of a summer thunderstorm, complete with sudden blasts of thunder coming from their lungs and flashes of lightning bolting from their eyes.

That generation of Martins and their in-laws were a tough, honest, hardworking, south Alabama farming family of preachers and pickers of cotton and guitars. They are my blood. They are part of the reason I am who I am.

Mama said she named me after Uncle Tommy, with both our middle names being Paul. It turned out being the honor for me that she had meant it to be.

Both Uncle Tommy and Daddy have now crossed the Jordan.

Daddy was not afraid of dying. I know that as a fact. I'd bet Uncle Tommy wasn't either. Both men felt that way because they knew they had earned a seat on that bus bound for Glory.

Both men were the type to look death square in the eye and never blink, then give it a sideways grin as Uncle Tommy hit the "Reaper" over the head with the closest Bible and Daddy poked it in the eye with his sixth finger.

Both men lived every day and drew every breath for the Lord. And when you're living life like that, how can you be afraid of dying?

I guess those flies were not afraid of dying either, or else they would have picked another porch to land on.

Grandpa didn't talk much. In fact, I don't remember him ever saying anything to me. Like most young boys, I had nothing to say worth listening to. Being an old man, he had plenty to say I needed to listen to—he just kept it a secret. But he liked to grab my ankle with the curve of his walking cane as I ran by. That's the same way he took a bent coat hanger to grab a chicken's leg so it could be caught, scalded, and plucked for Sunday dinner. When he caught me, I'd holler and squirm and he'd grin and hang on tight as if I were a young rooster bound for the glory of the cook pot.

Between grabbing my leg and spitting snuff juice in a coffee can, he did a good job of keeping the fly population in check. Of course, he had the help of fly tapes tacked and dangling from every ceiling like sticky stalactites. They not only caught flies, but caps and hairdos too.

I didn't realize at the time, but Granny and Grandpa would be the last of their kind. If I had, I would have paid closer attention and scribbled more notes in my mind. I didn't realize the world wouldn't be making any more like them. Not because of a shortage of parts, but because nobody seems to care much about quality anymore.

Houseflies, chickens and biscuits. Those are the main three of the many lasting memories I have of our trips to that house.

Eating Granny's biscuits was like what my childish imagination figured was a religious experience like Uncle Tommy and Daddy had—something you'd gladly give up most any sin for.

Anoint that biscuit with a little butter and you'd have non-believers lined up volunteering to say the blessing and thanking God.

I don't know what made her biscuits taste so good. But because of them, I thought Dothan, Alabama, was Heaven—or close enough that I could smell it from where I was standing on the porch—the porch where St. Peter was wearing suspenders and sitting at the gate, ready to grab my leg with his walking cane when I tried to sneak past him. Was it a secret biscuit recipe handed down to Granny from her Marchman mother? Or was it because her loving hands worked the dough in a carved wooden pan smoothed by generations of biscuit builders before her? The latter, I would imagine. And while we waited on Grandpa to say the blessing, these offspring of Martha White, Clabber Girl, hog lard, salt, buttermilk and water were anointed with butter, which taught me early on how to recognize a religious experience when I tasted one. Those "On The Eighth Day" creations were so cherished that sometimes a few would be left over.

Those were stashed in the screen-covered pie safe where they would lie in wait on a chance to have a thumb-hole poked in the top and the cavern filled with syrup—a grandchild's dream fulfilled and a confirmation that this old house was a place where at least one angel lived. But the adults had their own plans for any leftover biscuits—a plan that involved gravy made from coffee and ham drippings. I remember more than once getting my hand slapped for trying to sneak a biscuit. Mama would slap with the same vigor as when she caught me looking through the Sears catalog and pausing at the girdle page.

I remember watching over her shoulder as Granny racked flour from the banks of a buttermilk pond she'd poured in the middle of the bowl. Then she'd sprinkle salt and daub lard in the mix until it was just right. The dough couldn't be too thin or too thick, but just right to patty out and place onto a greased platter with just the right spacing where they'd be kissing by the end of the process, then the platter shoved into the oven to be drooled over later while the blessing was being said.

I don't know where that wooden biscuit bowl came from or where it ended up after Granny died. But wouldn't it be a shame if it were just sitting in a closet somewhere, gathering dust and not causing people to drool anymore.

The Walks

BIG WORDS

I DON'T REMEMBER ANY of the conversations, just the time we spent walking—just the steps.

I think maybe Daddy just needed to cleanse the paper mill from his system by passing through air that didn't smell like a lunch bucket full of boiled eggs. I think he was searching for his second wind, and I was tagging along.

I had to work hard to stay up with him. Not that he was walking fast or that his legs were long, it was just that mine were the normal length of a seven-year-old.

On these therapeutic Saturdays, we'd start out from the house, which was the last structure at the end of a dirt road that stopped at the edge of the woods.

From that spot where the road ended and my boyhood fantasy began, we'd take a narrow trail that meandered to no place in particular. A paved road now mimics the trail's original path, and it still meanders to no place in particular.

Daddy always walked in front of me. I guess he was just-in-case scouting for snakes. As I walked behind him, the broom sage brushed against my face and briars tried to pierce my denim covered legs. It was rare that those thorns ever succeeded. Britches were thicker in 1958. Or maybe I just don't remember any thorny encounters because it didn't matter.

My arms were a different story.

I'm not sure if blackberry bushes are bloodthirsty by nature or if the stickers are a prickly cover charge of sorts, the price you have to pay before you can go inside for the entertainment. In their youth, the berries are red like the lips of a honky-tonk queen and just as tempting. They come with a sour kiss that can pucker you like biting into a persimmon just one day before it's ripe. As I would one day learn, it takes a little maturity to turn the red berry into something more delicious; something that leaves you with a longing for another taste—be it berries or beauties.

I would come to realize that life, blackberries, and ladies are alike in that they can bring forth both pleasure and pain from the same encounter.

Like most males, no matter the age, I was a slow learner. So every few steps I would reach inside the blackberry bush again, searching for a better one.

By day's end, my lips and fingers were as black as a banker's heart and my arms were as scratched up as a hog that spent the day wallowing in a prickly pear patch.

Twenty-five yards past the blackberry thicket, the trail came to a foot log crossing a small creek. Well, I called it a creek. Really, it was a ditch dug by the county to drain the swamps in its losing battle to disrupt the mosquito orgies.

To the right of the foot log was a small area where the water pooled. That spot was a little cleaner looking and not as appealing to snakes as a place to hide and ambush frogs. Thinking back, it looked cleaner since it was less choked with algae and water lilies, thanks to hopeful fishermen and their crawfish drags.

A few years later, that spot would be where I'd spend many school days hiding. Each school morning when I left the house walking, I had one of two choices to make—I could turn left and walk toward the brick buildings around the corner and increase my public education or I could turn right and walk to the foot log and, well, increase my private education. On too many days, I turned right, which would have been the wrong direction and a "whoop'n" offense in Mama's eyes, if she'd seen me.

After rainy days, the water at the foot log was almost knee deep. A boy skipping school could take off his shoes and socks, roll up his britches legs and spend the day trying to trap crawfish that could run faster backwards than he could forward. Then that afternoon he could unroll his pants legs, put his socks and shoes back on, and go home innocent. And, except for the smell of stale mud, he'd try to appear to be dripping with knowledge gained inside that brick building, when really it was the sniffles from having his feet wet all day.

But those boyish pranks were still a few years away. Right now, Daddy and I were walking a foot log with our arms extended out sideways for balance, trying to get to the uphill side without falling in and so we could continue our walk with our feet dry. We tilted side to side, arms out, as we moved across the log. We looked like two crop dusters trying to land in a crosswind.

Sometimes, just for his entertainment, Daddy would pull a dried cicada shell clinging to the bark on a pine tree—a past life left behind by an old creature beginning a new adventure. Then, with the dried shell gently pinched between his thumb and trigger finger, he'd hook it to my ear.

"Now you can go to town cause you got'cha yo self a ear bob," he'd say and laugh.

The cicada's claws were bent just right to grab onto an earlobe and dangle like the ear decorations Miss Millie Ola at the drugstore wore.

Daddy called it a locust hull. It was something the new life had left behind as a reminder that you can walk away from an old life. It was like that old shell of a shanty Mama and Daddy left behind in Alabama after they moved to Florida. Daddy took me by that spot a few years later so I could see for myself what they left behind. It would be a memory that would stay with me for the rest of my life, like a locust hull dangling from my ear.

I guess that locust hull was kinda a metaphor for my future. Years later, with the help of a guitar, I would shed my shell, leaving the old me behind, just like that cicada did.

Daddy was a synonym for what Mama called "a good man." No beer drinking that I ever saw—or smelled, anyway. No cussing either, even after he stuck a screwdriver into the palm of his hand while prying open a stubborn oyster. I don't know why he never got himself a bona fide oyster knife. He rode to Port St. Joe every day to work. They could have stopped at a store any place in that bayside town where he could have bought one for a dollar. But to a survivor of "The Great Depression," why waste a dollar when you've got a screwdriver out of work and lying around in a spoon drawer?

As an adult, I still can't remember what we talked about on these excursions. I guess we'd just wander around and wonder about things, our brains not telling our feet what to do or how fast not to do it.

Although I don't remember our conservations, I do remember some things that happened, like when Daddy held my hand.

With him having six fingers on each hand, well, five fingers and a thumb, his grip should have felt different. Mama had held my hand plenty of times when she dragged me to church or into Dr. Canning's office to get my shots, so I knew what a normal hand felt like.

But Daddy's hand still felt normal to me. I guess because at that stage of my life, big words like polydactyly held the same inferior position of importance as the words "wash behind your ears."

When he was young, Daddy was ashamed of his hands. I came to that conclusion because in the only two pictures I have of him as a child, he is hiding his hands. Later in life, that uniqueness became his calling card, a way for the public to identify an honest, hard-working, God fearing man. "You know him," people would say. "That preacher man with six fingers on each hand."

I remember his hands felt rough. Later on, I realized why. Yes, he worked hard all his life, so his hands were callused. But also just as relevant was that a six-fingered work glove to protect his hands was, and still is, as rare as a watermelon tree.

On our walks, our first stop—other than the foot log which was more of a slowdown than a stop—was the ball field. It was finally getting lights installed for night games.

We stopped by there so I could peep over into the newly dug holes the diameter of a log truck tire. To a seven-year-old, the holes were dark, bottomless and probably had bats hanging around at the bottom, not the baseball kind either. Eventually giant treated poles would elevate bulbs and electricity and light up the field after dark. On Friday nights, we could sit on our porch and hear the cheers of high school football games that filled the air. And sometimes on Saturday nights, the circuit riding wrestlers would put on their shows there. So not only was the night air filled with whippoorwill calls but with Friday night cheers and Saturday night jeers.

Following my hole inspection, we'd continued puttering along a graded road that led to the Chipola River and Cochran's Landing. We considered that river the halfway point on our day of walking because that's where we turned around to start the trip back home.

At the landing, I would pick up small chunks of broken clay pottery and try to skip them across the tannic water. Because of all the pottery on the river bank, I thought there must have once been a Native American camp there. Later, I learned the truth, which, as usual, wasn't nearly as exciting as imagining scalps hanging on a stob. There was once a riverboat landing there. The chunks of pottery were used as old world styrofoam, cushioning the contents inside barrels and crates. They then sent those shipments around the river bend to places that, to me, only existed in my mind, or maybe on the map Daddy had wadded up and shoved into the car's glove box.

Before starting home, we'd set and rest on the roots of an old oak. I'd gaze up through the twisted limbs as we rested. These were rich times in my life; times when a twisted oak would be the closest thing to a spiral staircase I'd ever climb.

After resting a while, Daddy would find his second wind, and we'd walk home, mostly in silence, to once again approach the foot log crossing the creek.

With Daddy's system now cleansed from the paper mill smoke, and without saying a word, he would grab my hand as we approached that foot log. And once again, big words like polydactyly never crossed my mind.

Gone? Not Really

STACKED BY A WIND DEVIL

IT WAS THE BIGGEST hayloft I'd ever seen. It was the only hayloft I'd ever seen.

Up to that point, all that life had exposed me to was a smaller world made up of sagging tire swings and snuff-daubed wasp stings.

To me, the loft was colossal. It was like the whole outdoors, complete with the sound of birds, the smell of rat turds and the shed skin of a chicken snake. In one corner was a roll of old barbed wire with cattle hair still in its teeth as proof of its last meal. And over there were the wrinkled remains of a bumper crop of something other than dust. It was that big, this hayloft, as big as all outdoors. Unlike the natural outdoors, this one had a tin roof. But like all outdoors, it leaked when it rained.

I thought myself so brave, climbing those loose boards held together with spider webs and nails. Hand over hand I'd work to get up to the big room.

And I did it on my own without the help of a cousin double-dog-daring me to do it.

Once up there, I could look out through the hay door, a sort of hole in the present, and see across the gravel road, past the words "God Loves You" painted on a piece of tin leaning against a tree. Off in the distance, I could see the water tower in the nearby town of Enterprise, Alabama.

I was too young to fathom the concept, but from up there, even though I might not see my future through that hole, I could see my past.

The barn belonged to Mrs. Nett Strength and her late husband, Henry. He died in 1947, four years before my birth.

She wasn't kin by blood, but she could have passed for an aunt. Her old house was just up the hill from the barn. Even today, in my mind's eye, I can see her dressed in a pleated frock, wearing fogged-up eye glasses, watching over steaming pots of something magical with a spoon-shaped wand in her hand. Not only was she watching the pot boil, but she was also looking for a match to start a fire because soon it would be dark. She knew from experience that after the January sun went down, the old airy house had teeth, and it wouldn't hesitate to bite.

It was cold in the bedroom where I slept across the hall from the warmer kitchen. A colorful mountain of quilts buried me so deep that rolling over could work up a sweat bead on your forehead. And that was the last thing you needed when your forehead was about the only thing exposed to the icy wind that growled in through the cracks between the planks.

Funny. I don't remember being cold up there in that hayloft.

"Come down from up there and let's go for a walk." The voice came from the ground. It was Daddy. "I got sump'n to show you."

After walking for a while, he stopped and pointed to a small pile of rotting boards. The heap looked like a wind devil had stacked them while holding a grudge against at least one sharecropper named Daddy.

"That's where we lived when you were born," he said. It was as if he wanted me to understand just how far we had come from that termite tabernacle to our Jim Walter dream home back in North Florida. To Mama and Daddy that modest home was a castle wrapped in aluminum siding and well on its way to being paid off.

It was hard for my 10-year-old mind to reconstruct a house out of that pile of planks and promises of an easier life one day—a "one day" when bony mules, sore muscles and rainless summers didn't crowd out a man's dreams, a "one day" complete with paid vacations, Sundays off, and a company pension plan.

As we walked back toward Mrs. Nett's house, he stopped and pointed again. I followed his finger to a field full of weeds. But in his eyes, I could see that he saw more than a dream strangled by cockleburs and beggar lice. He saw more than I could ever see. "I used to plow that field behind a mule," he said with a look of relief on his face. "God answers prayers," he whispered, as if talking to himself. I didn't know what he meant then. I do now.

We rambled our way to the backyard, where an old bell still held its head high, propped up by two posts and an ivy vine.

"That's the bell Mrs. Nett would ring to call us in from the field to eat dinner," he said.

Other than sundown, that ringing in their ears was the only other relief they got from dancing the day away with cotton bolls and hot dirt trespassing through worn out soles. For the worn out souls between cotton rows where grit was the only bumper crop, the bell was music to their sweaty ears.

The house, the bell, the barn, the boards, the planks and the promises... the history of that past and that place that is now gone, replaced by an airport, I am told.

But is it really gone as long as the memories of a few stragglers are hanging on and passing it on to grandkids too young to fathom the concept of being able to see the past through a hole in the present?

I say no, it won't be gone. Daddy saw to that for at least one more generation. It's now up to me.

The Mocking Bird

SOUNDS LIKE SIN TO ME

According to Daddy and Atticus Finch, killing a mockingbird was a sin.

In fact, to Daddy, killing most any bird was a sin. Except a chicken. It was okay to kill a chicken, especially if a preacher was coming for dinner. The Bible says so in 1 Timothy 5-16, "The laborer deserves his wages."

Daddy read his Bible, but I'm pretty sure he never read Harper Lee's *To Kill a Mockingbird*. So I don't know where he got the idea it was a sin to kill a mockingbird.

In Lee's book, Atticus told Scout that the mockingbird represented innocence. That made it a sin to kill one because you were destroying innocence. Sure sounds like a sin to me.

I would have thought it was a bottle of whiskey or the back seat of a '62 Chevy that destroyed innocence, not a Daisy BB gun with a songbird in its sights and a nervous finger on the trigger. But what did I know? I was just a boy wanting to impress his father.

Saying I was proud of myself would have been like calling the Grand Canyon a low spot in the road. I had squatted and crawled, managed and maneuvered so the wind would be in my face and the target wouldn't get a whiff of a nervous boy. It looked at me. I stopped. Held my breath, then inched forward again until I got close to the plum tree where the mockingbird sat singing on a low limb. All that maneuvering paid off. There was no way I would miss from here. I didn't miss. The mockingbird was as surprised as I was. The sweet taste of success was on my tongue.

I couldn't wait to show it off to Daddy. The lifeless feathered shades of gray and white drooped over the sides of my hand as I ran into the house to show off my Daniel Boone skills. That's when he—without scolding or anger—told me what he thought about it. "Poor bird will never sing again," Daddy said. "You know God knows when every sparrow falls. I'm sure he knows when mockingbirds fall, too." The sweet taste of success was now as bitter as a dose of Black Draught.

A study by people who ought to know found that mockingbirds are unique. Besides mimicking the calls of other birds and man-made noises like music and machinery, the mockingbird can imitate at least twelve different species of frogs and toads. Now that's a proficient polyglot.

There are a bunch of honky-tonk troubadours who'd pin a Pamper on a polecat to have a repertoire like that.

I doubt mockingbirds have a song list to go by—unlike most musicians. They sing whatever song comes to mind.

When I play music, we do have a list of which song comes next. Sure, the lineup sometimes changes depending on how the dancers are responding. Maybe a line dance, followed by a two-step, followed by a slow song. Sometimes two slow songs in a row if the dance floor Casanova's with honey on their tongues and mischief on their minds need more time for their lies to ferment or the brawling pot starts to boil and the rougher hotheads need cooling off with a touch of smooth George Jones.

Hand a song list to a mockingbird and see how far that gets you. He sings what he pleases when he pleases, whether or not it pleases his listeners.

The mockingbird and I have at least one thing in common—we both sing songs others have sung before us, nothing original.

What Daddy told me that day wasn't original either. He had heard it from somebody. His words, no matter the source, have stuck with me. And I don't remember ever again killing another mockingbird—in fact any other songbird in cold blood. Yes, I have "grilled" a few low-slow flyers with the front end of a truck, but I didn't mean to.

Now, killing a chicken, that's a different story. Maybe they need to learn how to sing.

Unseen Force

THE ESCAPE

THE SPARROW FLEW ABOVE Daddy's head as he preached from the pulpit of that single-room, cinder block tabernacle in Kinard, Florida, where he was the pastor.

It was a frosty morning, so we got there before everyone else. The early arrival gave Daddy a chance to build a fire in the wood stove that had a prominent spot near the front pew.

Putting it there was a clever way to get folks to sit up front instead of on the chilly back pew—for one season, anyway.

The sparrow was still there when the service started, fluttering around the small building, brushing up against the hallelujahs that floated to the ceiling. He also had to dodge a few "King James" verses shot from the barrel of a Bible by a dead-eye preacher who sent "shalt nots" ricocheting from wall to wall, ceiling to floor. If asked, the sparrow wouldn't have agreed, but he was better off inside with the "holy rollers" than outside with the hungry cats.

Now and then, in desperation, the confused bird would lower a wing and make a dive for a window, only to slam into the pane—and the pain—with a thud. Since he saw his reflection in the glass, I guess he thought it was another sparrow on the outside showing him how to get out. But it was just a ghost of himself, caught in a quandary of trying to get in while trying to get out. Since God knows when every sparrow falls, you would think that He would also know when one is bumping into a pane and lay it on somebody's heart to walk over and open the window. I guess nobody's heart was listening. I know mine wasn't. It was too busy wishing I could get away, too.

Every head-jarring encounter with the glass reminded him that a force that he could not see was keeping him from flying away. He would end up going to church that day, whether or not he wanted or needed to. It looked like he was bound to become a bird of pray, for that one day, anyway.

I watched and wondered if he, like me, was just a wanderer wanting to get away and follow his nature instead of being stuck in a hallelujah hoedown with a preacher who was determined to take off his Bible belt and whip the Devil out the front door, no matter how long it took

As I daydreamed out the window, I could see my reflection. It was also running into a force that I could not see that kept me from flying away.

In my case, the force was Mama's unbending belief that all boys should be in church every time the door was open, whether or not they wanted or needed to be.

Or was it that my reflection, like the sparrow's, represented something much more significant than just a refraction of the present situation—something deeper? Like maybe our dual desire to escape from something we could not see or understand and didn't want to see or understand, not on a clear Sunday, when there were better things to do outside.

After the hallelujahs had settled to the floor and the dollar bill in the collection plate was counted and recorded in the church ledger, Daddy opened up a "window of opportunity" for the sparrow. He left the window open as we loaded into the car and went home. No worries about leaving a window open. It wasn't like someone was going to crawl through it and steal valuables from the church—in this case the most valuable thing in the church was the firewood.

The following Sunday the sparrow was gone. We never saw him again. I guess he figured he had enough religion to last him the rest of his life. Birds of a feather. I wish I could fly.

A few months later, my first guitar came in the mail. My parents ordered it from a Sears Roebuck catalog. I forget which page number.

Just think, if we'd had an outhouse, I might not have become a guitar picker because that catalog page might have been missing come mail-order day. My musical career could have been wiped out before it even got started. Lucky for me we had indoor plumbing. I could thank a commode for my musical career.

The guitar was a Silvertone acoustic. It came with Black Diamond strings that would eat the tips of your fingers like a 6-strand barbed wire fence would do if you were trying to play "Wildwood Flower" between the fence posts. Daddy's calluses were on his hands. Mine were on the tips of my fingers.

But really, it doesn't matter where your calluses are located, work is still work. And learning to play that Silvertone was work.

As if by premonition, the guitar was the color of a wall in a room that got its light from neon. It had a smoky-colored pickguard surrounding a round "hole in the wall." There was no glass in that hole either, so like a sparrow through an open church window, a boy could escape, if he wanted. The fretboard didn't smell like smoky fingers either—not yet, anyway. At that time, I still knew nothing about dimly lit, smoky rooms. Mama and Daddy prayed I would stay ignorant.

I didn't beg for that guitar like I later did for a motorcycle, and it wasn't Christmas when my folks handed it to me. So the only life event I can think of that might merit such a gift was my coming of age—a time when my parents recognized that the music that was already in my blood was about to heat up.

They had to figure that I would follow my heritage and play music, so they'd better point me in the right direction early on. At least that way they might have an influence on which musical fork in the road I took when the light changed from stop to go.

The road's right fork led to the church around the corner. The left fork led to the juke joint between our house and Honeyville. It was a place where people preached, cussed, and a few "cats" hungry for brighter lights were cursed with the ability to make guitars talk. It was the place where the hangovers hung out. A few people there could even tell you what the dance floor and the bouncer's fist tasted like.

Like most musicians, for a while I took both roads. First, I played for the altar call for Jesus at the church. From there I played for "last call for alcohol" for the regulars at the dance hall.

Unfortunately, if you want to make a living playing the guitar and dazzle folks in the process, the right fork is the wrong fork. That leaves only the left fork, which turned out to be my right fork.

Life can be so confusing sometimes. A boy doesn't know whether to fly out a window to the place where the "cool cats" congregate or stay inside where it's safe. But no matter whether he ended up in church or in a bar, his faithful traveling companion was always his guitar.

What else could I have done? It's hard to win when you are arm wrestling with genetics. Daddy played. Uncle Ed played. Uncle Tommy played. My first cousins Janice, David, Joe Mac, Jim, Mike and Faron played. So I guess my parents figured I'd play too.

From the moment I was born in Coffee County, Alabama, my heart was already beating in three-quarter time to the tune of Hank's "Lonesome Whippoorwill."

Music could not help but be a part of me and me a part of it. It was in the red dirt in Alabama where I was born. It was in the river waters around Wewahitchka, Florida, where I swam. It was in the walls at my school, from Mrs. Shirley's second grade class where she played her autoharp to Mr. Semmes' FFA band and his constant request for us to play "Under The Double Eagle" just one more time. As scratchy as it sounded, music was also in that first record player Daddy bought—the one I listened to when I tried to figure out how to play a song; the one that had the nickel taped to the playing arm to keep it from skipping. Sometimes, after running in circles for a while, a nickel wasn't enough. Then Daddy would have to raise the ante to a quarter unless he wanted to listen to Jimmie Davis skip through "Suppertime."

And music was also in the cinder blocks of that church in Kinard. I just didn't hear it for the shouting. I don't think Daddy could hear it either. If he had, he might not have ordered that Sear's guitar and opened that "window of opportunity" that I would one day fly out of, like a sparrow just trying to escape so he can do what birds were meant to do.

Holy Rollers

ONE OF THOSE CHURCHES

When you go to an old timey holiness church for the first time, don't expect a quiet encounter with God.

A high-octane holiness church is a place where God does not tippy-toe around. Nope, he kicks open the door, barges in and runs around the room, stepping over non-padded pews and around believers strewn across the floor. This sprawling of foot washers on the floor is called "slain in the spirit" where a simple touch to the forehead by a fire-breathing apostle can drop believers as if they'd been run over by a bus bound for glory. There were sometimes half a dozen men and women, all sprawled out like on a dance-hall floor after a brawl—only without the blood, the teeth on the floor, and the hard feelings. Some were shaking, while others were speaking in tongues as the Holy Spirit flowed through them.

People call them "holy rollers," this jubilant bunch of followers of that old time religion. Yes, when they "get happy," they will jump and shout and even roll around on the floor despite the threat of being stumbled over. Some people say the term "holy rollers" is derogatory. Others say it's a badge of honor—almost like a Purple Heart for having their hands stepped on during Wednesday prayer service.

Gospel singer, the late Andrae Crouch, once said, "They call us holy rollers, and what they say is true. But if they knew what we were rollin' about, they'd be rollin' too."

At least there were no snakes involved. not at the churches where I played music.

All I can figure is that these sermonizing sky pilots must think God is hard of hearing. That's why they feel the need to holler and shout and throw down their microphones because it ain't loud enough. That piece of modern technology only gets in the way and muffles the message. Besides, it's hard to gallop down an aisle when you're attached to a mic chord and it is attached to a static-driven Fender amp plugged into a wall.

Growing up, I went to one of "those" churches, so I just assumed all churches were that way. That is until I went to my first Baptist church service.

Susan and I had just started dating. I went to her church that Sunday morning, not because I felt I needed to, but because she did. About all I remember about the service is thinking, "Dang, at our church we make more noise at a funeral!" Susan's dad was a deacon there. He sat on a front pew and kept turning around, looking at us. I figured he was checking on my safety—just making sure the roof hadn't fallen on my head. It was so quiet in there that I heard someone's stomach growling just after noontime as a signal to the preacher that it was time for him to wrap it up.

Daddy was a "holy roller" preacher who didn't wear a watch and preached in a room where they could not have heard a pulpwood truck sporting a holey muffler crank up in the parking lot, much less a stomach singing the blues. He was a bona fide Disciple of Decibels—dedicated to the extreme. On more than one occasion, our family had been in our Chevy, stuck in a muddy ditch along a deserted clay road somewhere between Heaven's gate and Hell's back door. We were on our way to a country church where, if you didn't count yourself and your family, there would have been more mosquitoes inside seeking salvation than people. I've played in clubs that were the same way.

Daddy had answered the call to preach, and nobody said anything about there being a crowd to listen. So he preached to the ones who showed up. Oh boy, did he! He could peel paint off a wall with his glare when he looked up between reading scriptures. This verse reading was the pulpit prelude to a sermon that would soon have the Devil seeking a cooler place. When Daddy looked you in the eye, it was as if he could look right through you and see every sin you ever committed, or thought about committing. It made me want to look at the floor to keep from revealing myself.

From his look on one particular Sunday morning, I figured he already knew about it, so I came within a gnat's breath of confessing before he even asked me about it. To me, it was no big deal that our bass player and I had gone into the church after dark and "borrowed" amps to use at a dance hall on a Saturday night. No big deal. What was there to confess? We had them back before daylight Sunday morning, early enough that we figured no one was awake to catch us, especially on a Sunday. We figured even God was sleeping in that morning after being up late, watching over us at Mama's request.

I'm glad now that I didn't confess because I don't think Daddy ever knew. The church folks didn't either. They would have frowned at the knowledge that their church amps had been wallowing in sin right up to our last call and about four hours before their altar call. Unlike the night before, I was glad that the 1965 Fender Twin Reverb was quiet and kept its sins to itself.

These holiness folks take their religion seriously and straight on the rocks with nothing added to flavor it up or water it down. They made religion fun! Comparing their services to other denominational services would be like comparing an earthquake to a "bench rattler." Sunday church goers will know what that is, and that's why you never eat dry beans on Saturday night.

Back in the 60s, holiness was a middle class religion. No "big shots," like mayors or city commissioners, attended our church. They liked the quieter sanctuaries in town.

Ours was a working class congregation made up of pulpwooders, mill workers, roofers, house painters and wives who worked at home and in school lunchrooms. These were women whose hands still stung on Sunday morning from picking okra, and their backs still ached from being stooped over picking butter beans.

A few of the women dipped a little snuff, and most of the men chewed a little tobacco. And at least one man's breath smelled like Listerine—a cloaking method to keep rumors from getting started about old Bro So-in-So falling off the wagon again.

But I don't believe a little dark sinning shaded their bright goodness in the eyes of their Savior. My precious grandmother dipped snuff, and she convince me long ago that there would be spit cans in Heaven.

Dipping snuff might not have been a sin to these women, but wearing ragged clothes to Sunday school was. You saw no raveled and ragged edges on young'uns clothes, not on The Lord's Day.

But you might just see a frayed edge or two at the Wednesday night prayer meeting service. A devil-may-care Wednesday wasn't as formal and sin-less as Sunday.

The preachers didn't care what you wore. "Wearing clothes with holes in 'em ain't no reason to bow your head in shame," he said. "But if you treat your neighbor poorly because he's walking around barefooted... now that's a reason to hang yo head so you can see if yo shoes are untied!"

They were not poor. They were not rich either. They were somewhere in the middle, bobbing around life like a cork on a line with a minnow hook. They had little chance of catching anything bigger than a pint-size paycheck, even after a work week deserving of a quart. But they were poor enough to know that the Bible printers could have saved money and ink by leaving out the verse about how hard it is for a rich man to get into Heaven. They didn't need that in their Bibles because being rich wouldn't be what kept them out of Heaven. But cussing at 16-hour days of sweating might. The way they had it figured, if hard work was a poor person's genocide, then they'd just get to Heaven a little sooner.

But despite all the hard work involved with "just get'n by," I never heard them complain. As a group, they enjoyed life. They figured it was okay to not have much money as long as you didn't have too many regrets to go along with it. The problem was, having even a few regrets usually involved a sin or two. But most didn't mind a preacher pointing out those sins on a Sunday as long as he didn't rub their noses in it. Besides, to them, a minor sin was like a tick on a dog's ear: leave it alone and it will eventually fall off by itself. It didn't need a preacher pulling on it every Sunday for that to happen.

Families made up most of the congregation. Children would be asleep on pallets laid out on the floor between pews. These colorful quilts were as old and worn as the deacon's excuse for missing church last Sunday. He could say what he wanted, but everybody knew the river level was just right and the brim were biting.

The teenage boys sat on the back two pews. We were in straight rows and looked and smelled like weeds sprayed with Hai Karate that had sprouted up in Heaven's flower bed. I had answered the altar call and gone up front a few times. Most times it was according to how bad the preacher had scared me, or which girl had gone up front. But I had backslid by the time I slid back to my seat.

To set the record straight, I had and still have the utmost respect for these "holy rollers" and what they believe. They believe something better is awaiting them beyond the grave; something better than lugging around a McCulloch chainsaw that won't start; something better than a mill threatening to cut them off or put them on a quota;

something better than a skipping Chevy in need of new tires and an oil change; something better than greedy bankers waiting on the needy's porch.

To them, the grave held no secrets or regrets. That by itself was, and still is, reason enough to be rolling around on the floor!

Get A Real Job

DONKEY DUMPING TRASH

As far as I know, Daddy was the only one in his family who played a musical instrument. He could make a Hohner harmonica sound more lonesome than a yonder train whistle after midnight. Mama said he used to play at square dances. I remember him playing and singing in church.

"When I Take My Vacation in Heaven" replaced "Orange Blossom Special" as his favorite song.

Not only could he "choke a harp" and sing, but in between he could fling and sling scriptures at you like horseshoes. His aim was good, too. He would have the Devil ducking and two-stepping, slamming the door behind him as he ran out into the church parking lot, looking for something cool to drink.

Because of my family tree, I could have been a preacher. But I took a different fork in the tree when climbing down and wound up playing in jukes.

Though he said nothing to me about it, I knew Daddy didn't approve of my honky tonking. In jest, I would tease him about it. "I'll take care of 'em on Saturday night," I'd say. "You take care of 'em on Sunday morning." My mission on Saturday night was to help people forget about the past week they'd spent in their hellish jobs. His mission on Sunday morning was to remind a few of those same people they would spend a lot longer than a week in hell if they didn't get in step with the Lord.

Not once did he preach to me about how he and I were on different pages in life's book. Mama was different. She wasn't about to let my being grown stop her from baptizing me in her opinion.

"You need to get out of them places and get yo'self a real job," she said more than once.

"Mama, I have a job. I get paid to play."

"Yea, and you using that money to buy gas for the devil's Cadillac," she said. "And you know full well where that fancy car's gonna take ya!"

She wasn't finished yet.

"Dem honky tonks are a sinner's trough," she said. "And here you are fillin' it with music so they can belly up to it. Get a good job."

Still, she wasn't finished.

"I'm jes trying to keep you from slipp'n into that 'Lake of Fire,' while dem honky tonkers are trying their best to push you in it."

To her, a "real job" meant logging or pulpwooding, railroading or even worm grunting. It could be anything other than bending guitar strings so sinners could backslide while Haggard sang in their ears about "mixing misery and gin." Mama didn't like it one iota that I worked in places where they dusted the dance floor with a layer of Hoover's Fine Ground Cornmeal so the slow dancers could glide like they were waltzing on air. Then put a second dusting of Hoover's Medium Ground so the buck dancers could scoot like they were wearing roller skates, their bottom half looking like a runaway train while their top half looked like a Sunday ride in the country. Corn meal just made it easier for people to backslide without getting their feet tangled in their morals.

Sometimes I wondered if my soul's destination was really Mama's concern. Or was it just how it didn't look right for the son of a preacher to be standing on smoky stages, bending "strangs" on a Fender "getar" so people could drink whiskey like they were getting paid to do it—like it was their real job.

"That's the same kinda places your Uncle Ed plays in," she said.

Edsel Martin is Mama's baby brother. He also took a different fork while climbing down from the family tree. She would preach to him too about how the path to Heaven and the path to hell look a lot alike except for that one fork in the tree.

Uncle Ed was a fine guitar player in a family of fine guitar players. To me, he was a legend who had gazed out across his and somebody else's share of stormy dance floors. For decades he played his Gretsch guitar in these hazy havens where young women with yellow hair and white teeth and old men with white hair and yellow teeth were all looking for a way to forget.

As Southern tradition dictated, they also coated those dance floors in corn meal to help add wings to brogans and sashay to stilettos.

Carpet cushioned the walls in these places where drinking had more to do with quenching hurt than it did with quenching thirst. It was a place where you paid to walk in the front door and could get thrown out the back door for free.

The shagged walls were painted in Marlboro brown and filled with the authentic moans of a troubled singer who sounded like Hank Sr. himself.

That true Southern sound reached every corner by way of cheap microphones sizzling like an egg frying as the music crackled through hand-me-down amps that hummed, but did it in tune with the music. Everybody there had a good time despite knowing that the next day their mamas would plead for them to "get out of them places" because it just didn't look right. Mamas have always been sticklers for appearances. My mama was no different.

But her rules didn't apply only to honky tonks. More than once she pressured Daddy to call the law after our drunk neighbor fell off his donkey in the middle of the dirt road in front of our house.

The donkey, our neighbor's main mode of transportation, would run away braying while Mama was praying that he'd come back and "pick up the trash" he'd dumped in the road.

This man was a good man. He just got thirsty a lot. It seems the beer bottles had reached a point where they just couldn't make it through the day without him. That thought, along with his designated donkey driver, left a nasty taste in Mama's morals.

"That donkey done dumped that man in the middle of the road again," she'd tell Daddy in a tone that sounded like someone dumping out a slop jar. "Call Preacher."

Johnathon (Preacher) Glass was the entire police force of Wewahitchka, Florida.

From history, Preacher knew that the neighbor always rode double with bad luck and often lost his balance right in front of our house on his way home. It happened the same way, everytime. When he and the donkey reached our newspaper box, the neighbor would tip over the donkey's right shoulder until gravity overwhelmed him. I don't care how much you've had to drink, it's hard to miss the ground...

and he didn't. Once there, he'd pass out face down in a tire rut. I doubt he felt his run-in with Mother Earth until the next day.

"Woodrow!" Mama said. "What will people think, a man drunk and passed out right here in front of a preacher's house?"

At least now, for a little while anyway, her focus was on the neighbor. That took the pressure off me to get out of those sin-filled places and "get a good job." It made me glad that I had bought him that quart of beer the night before because it turned out to be an advance payment for his sinning running interference for mine.

It's All In The Delivery

NON-VERBAL COMMUNICATION

I DON'T REMEMBER THE message from many of those endless holiness sermons about living sinless lives. As a child, I dozed and daydreamed through most of them. Mama made me sit next to her on those unpadded pews tempered by time and held together from the bottom with Juicy Fruit chewing gum as hard as Mama's stares when I wouldn't be still.

Though I remember little of what was said, I remember squirming through the sermons, trying to keep my dangling feet from going to sleep. If my feet went to sleep, I knew it wouldn't be long before the drowsiness worked its way up to my eyes. Boy howdy! I didn't want that to happen. If I closed my eyes, I'd have a "wake up" pinch coming.

If there had been a contest for such things, Mama, who was a better-than-average pincher, would have won "The Crawdad Award." Those critters can grab you pretty tight, too.

This pinching was non-verbal communication with a message as clear as a baby's conscience—stay awake!

The quieter preachers at the steepled churches in town could've learned something from Mama—the secret to having your message remembered is all in the delivery.

I might not recall all that was hollered at me from the pulpit, but I remember it had a common theme that echoed Mama's mantra: you can either go to church and not squirm or can go to Hell where you'll have plenty to squirm about. "And I won't be there to stop you," Mama said with her chin pointed toward Heaven.

Though I might not recall the message, I remember the messengers.

Those men of God were on fire and could make you feel Hell's heat. It was as if someone had opened an oven door in the back of the sanctuary. You could smell the sin going up in smoke.

The worship services were loud and long. Unlike a Baptist Bible thumper, a holiness never quite figured out that a sermon half as long was twice as good.

These services were seldom uneventful.

People would get happy and jump up and ride the backs of pews like a trick rider on a wooden horse. Though the pews could get a little wobbly, the riders never got bucked off, not even once. That made me think God must have been involved and was holding them up by the scruff of their sweaty shirts.

Women had their waist-length hair twisted and piled on top of their heads, like a conglomeration of beehive and bouffant. When they'd "get happy," they'd sling their heads so hard that their hair would uninstall itself as dozens of metal bobby pins hit the floor. It sounded like someone had spilled a bag of Skittles.

People would start running toward the altar, crying as they hastened because the preacher had scared the hell right out of their hearts and the Devil was chasing them, trying to reclaim what was once his.

Sometimes just to get to the altar was almost like fighting your way through the crowd at the rasslin' matches just to go buy a Dr. Pepper. But in this case, the church altar was the confession stand, not the concession stand.

With much of the crowd now around the altar, the preacher would continue as he zeroed in on those of us who stayed seated in the pews. I can remember that part real clear.

"YOU BETTER STAY OUTTA THEM JUKE JOINTS," he would scream with eyes that spewed fire and a tongue that spit nails and broken glass. "PEOPLE GO TO DEM BARS LOOKING FOR SOMEONE TO LEAN ON. CAN I GET'A AMEN? THEN WHEN THEY GET THERE, THEY FIND OUT THAT EVERYBODY IS ALREADY LEANING. WELL GLORY! LEAN ON THE LORD. HE DON'T NEED NO PROP."

Pulling out a red bandana, he'd wipe his forehead, then wave the damp cloth in the air as if he was trying to flag down the Greyhound to Gloryland.

Then he always seemed to look right at me as if he were a fortune teller. "USE THEM GETARS TO DRIVE PEOPLE TO CHURCH, NOT TO DRIVE THEM TO DRINK!"

When I was older, if a preacher started talking like that, I'd remember something I needed to take care of outside. I'd squirm like I used to and think about following the Devil out the door to the parking lot.

If Mama could have reached the back pew, I know what she would have done.

Disappointment? I Hope Not

MAGIC WITHOUT A HAT OR A RABBIT

To sooth her winter doldrums, around midsummer Mama stuffed a sweet potato into a quart jar of water sitting on the kitchen windowsill. It wasn't to one day eat. It was to one day look at.

By January, its dangling green vines would add warm color to a cold view of winter looming on the other side of the frosted window.

But no need for melancholy thoughts. Soon it would be spring and once again the red birds would sit in the azalea bush just outside that same window, looking in at Mama as she's looking out at them.

Suddenly, in a burst of energy, they spook. It is as if someone had shot a gun or a cat had strolled by.

In the flutter of chaos, it looked as if some of the red and pink azalea blooms had taken flight against a blue sky and just disappeared. It was like being in the middle of a delightful dream and the dog barks, spooking you awake, turning your castle on a hill back into a Jim Walter house on cinder blocks.

Mama loved cardinals. Especially the males with their blood-red plumage. They were the perfect, beautiful contrast to most anything mankind could throw together in a world that sometimes seemed to lose its color and soul.

With my mind's eye, I can still see her busy at the counter, hard at work. Good cooking has never been easy. Playing in my head like a reel from a silent movie, I watch her kneading dough and rolling it flat, then into a disk using an empty syrup bottle. When the glob reaches the right thickness that she measures with a glance, she folds it in half, careful not to break it, lifts it up as if picking up a baby and unfolds it over a pie pan like it was a cradle.

The drooping edges look like flour-white shingles hanging over the side of a metal roof. She shaves the excess off with a knife Daddy made for her out of an old crosscut saw blade. I think it might have been an anniversary gift that followed them from Alabama.

Using a spoon, she creates ornamental indentations around the top edge. This gives the pies a little eye flare and makes people wonder if Daddy got a raise and we are now part of the fancy folks who buy their crust ready-made from the IGA.

Thank God she wasn't frying beef tripe that day or I would have missed it all. I hated that smell and found something to do outside—way outside and upwind—whenever she was cooking it.

This pie-making smelled nothing like sizzling cow innards. Comparing the two would be like comparing the smell of a doughnut shop to the smell of a truck-stop bathroom. So I stayed in the kitchen, sniffing and hoping to get in a lick on a dripping beater before she tossed it into the dishpan.

This taste of lemony heaven topped in egg-white meringue wasn't destined for our table. But who knows, a young feller might still get a bowl to lick out if he's patient and don't ask too many questions.

Mama didn't have time for questions. She was busy making good on her pledge of pies to be sold by the church ladies raising money for the "building fund." In other kitchens strung out across town, other like-minded ladies were doing the same thing. They were like a cavalry of God's soldiers wearing print dresses and aprons that didn't match.

To watch Mama work was like watching magic unfold before my eyes without the aid of a hat or a rabbit.

Her goal—their goal—was to turn flour, sugar and eggs into money, and that money into a brand new cinder-block building where Jesus could come and visit at least twice a week, on Wednesdays and Sundays.

With the ladies' help, the building drive paid off. While their accomplishment wasn't as dramatic as turning water into wine, it was close. They turned white dough into green dough. They paid for the cinder blocks, the building went up and indeed God showed up twice a week—probably on the other nights too, when nobody was there to see.

And if an infidel looking for a sideshow didn't believe in miracles, he could grab a back pew on a Wednesday night and see for himself. There he might just come to change his mind. Then he could walk away with pie on his face, God in his heart, wondering why he ever doubted the starch in the hearts of these ladies wearing print dresses and aprons that didn't match.

Sometimes Mama would cry as she worked her hands and stared out the frosty window at red birds only she could see. I never knew why she cried. I never asked and regret that I didn't. She wouldn't have told me, anyway. She would have just shooed me outside with a fib, telling me she was about to fry Daddy some beef tripe.

I wonder if she was crying because something had spooked her dreams during the bloom of her life and those dreams had taken flight and disappeared? Or was it worry about whether payday would get here in time?

Maybe it was just chagrin dripping off her chin because I didn't know my spelling words, or she feared I might one day play music in "them places," her synonym for juke joints. Maybe she was just homesick for Alabama and was just missing her mama. The odds were in favor of her having to deal with at least some melancholy that even a sweet potato vine just couldn't soothe.

But disappointment? I hope not.

Thank God For Sinners

STUCK IN AN ALABAMA DITCH

THREE OF US WERE still sitting in the car after the tractor dragged us up to the church. Daddy was standing near the front of the car, talking to our liberator.

We were still seated the way we were when we left home that morning in our white like-new, '62 Chevy Bel Air. Mama was riding shotgun and my brother and I were in the back seat. Daddy had got out to pay the man, but the man refused to take it. He just got back on his tractor and followed the sloshy ruts back toward his house to wait on the next load of wayfaring strangers.

We were in south Alabama on a soggy dirt parking lot in front of a white-washed, cinder-block Assembly of God church. It was stained green on one side by a nearby oak tree, and orange on the other side from road residue during dustier times of the year. Our car was still a '62 Chevy, but not white anymore. Now it was a washed-out red, even the windshield, except where the wipers had scraped off enough red mud so Daddy could peep through to aim. That Bel Air looked like it had been "washed in the blood," just like the choir back home sang about on page #238 of the church songbook.

Somewhere near Cottonwood, Alabama, is where we were. I didn't know the exact where. I'm not sure Daddy did either. And that could be an important piece of information when you're stuck in a ditch and needing to call for help. That is, if you could find something to call on and someone to call out to.

Daddy never said how he found this church. But I remember saying to myself at a volume only I could hear, "What in the world would the Lord be doing way out here this far away from the paved road?" Daddy didn't hear what I said. But the Lord might have.

There had been a thunderstorm the previous night. The rain seemed to contain that owl "stuff," and we've all heard about how slick that stuff is.

Somewhere along Alabama 53, across from a juke joint with a blinking Falstaff sign that was sort of Daddy's guiding North Star, we turned onto a narrow dirt road. Funny, blinking signs like that would one day be my North Star, too. I just didn't know it right then.

We made it about halfway to the church when the front of the car started wandering, and I'm sure Daddy started wondering if we'd make it or not. We slid to the right and right into the ditch, almost hitting a mailbox with the red flag up, waiting on Monday's mailman to slide to a stop there.

Mama grabbed the dash and Daddy gunned the gas as the Chevy jumped out of the ditch and slid across the road and into the other ditch. Daddy gunned it again. In a sacrilegious reaction, the Bible on the dash slid to the floor. Empty Coke bottles clanged together on the back floorboard, singing and ringing as the front and rear of the car tried to swap places. Mama prayed. "Lord, please don't let nothing happen to us 'cause nobody'll ever find us way out here buried in this Alabama mud."

Daddy wrestled with the steering wheel as if it were a drunk goat he had by the horns.

The goat slipped out of Daddy's hands and we veered right again. My brother and I slid into the left door, our heads almost clanging together like the bottles under our feet. Mama continued to pray. The Bible slid under her seat as if it were hiding from a drunk goat.

The Chevy came to rest in the right ditch, leaning against a rusty barbed-wire fence. One strand was strung across the hood.

We were stuck and the only house nearby was the one we'd slid by a few seconds ago, almost hitting their mailbox. I figured our only hope of being found would be if a descendent of Noah's crow might spot us as he was flying around, looking for a dry spot where he could land without bogging up or down.

As if it were a routine he was accustomed to, the old man who lived in the house was already walking out the door to save us. Save us, that is, if his tractor would start.

I don't know how our savior wearing overalls knew we were in the ditch. It was not from a cell phone call from Daddy, not back then. Back then, my cousin was the only person I knew who had ever used a cell phone—the jailer had handed him the receiver between the bars.

Looking back now, I figure the old man must have had guineas that ran toward the house, sounding the alarm as we slid past the mailbox. Guineas are good at loud overreactions when they see a Chevy skidding by in the ditch.

No matter how he found out, we were glad to see him, his Ford 9N that did start, and his chain.

"All y'all okay?" he said, looking down at us and spitting over the tractor tire.

His straw halo had the same red mud around the brim as the car rims. His jaw bulged, not from a bovine kick, but from a chew of Bull of the Woods. As an appetizer, he had a non-filter Camel "ready-roll" between his lips. The renegade smoke caused him to squint one eye as he looked over this pitiful scene. His open eye mirrored a hard life. He smelled like Listerine and Old Spice. Years later, I learned that those teamwork aromas were an old standby for masking the smell of the previous night's merriment. There was also a third aroma I recognized, so I figured someone in his life must have sold Avon.

I heard him grumble something about "city folk" in a low voice, while taking the Lord's name in vain. I figured he wasn't a holiness "foot-washer" who had planned to show up in overalls that morning to hear Daddy preach. Nope. He was just an everyday sinner with a logging chain and a tractor, so that made him a welcome sinner in my book. But who am I to judge? He could have just as well been one of God's sheep in a wrinkled shirt, helping a load of wayfaring strangers to get to church on time.

Since that day, I've seen plenty of angels a lot rougher around the edges than him. They cross our paths as friendly reminders that we are all rough sawn in the beginning and just trying to whittle down the sharp edges so maybe we won't become a splinter in someone's life.

This trip to Alabama was nothing new. Daddy took us on a lot of these lost-soul roundups when I was young. I called it his "Footwashers Tour." Sometimes we would end up being the ones lost and in need of saving and needing the mud washed off our feet.

I'd witnessed one footwashing when I was a boy sitting on the back pew.

The preacher set two chairs near the altar. A man would sit in one, a woman in the other. Both were barefooted and had their feet in a washpan of water. The men folk would line up in front of the man and the women in the other line. Then each one would take turns washing feet. Each person had a turn sitting in the chair to have their feet washed. I'm not sure, but I think the ritual's intent was for Christians to humble themselves in the sight of the Lord. As a viewer, I remember thinking that, unlike my feet, their feet were already clean and didn't really need washing. But what did I know, being a teenager and not knowing much about humility?

On his "Footwashers Tour," Daddy operated on the principle that you had to take the preaching to the sinner, and he figured south Alabama had just as many sinners as north Florida.

The Cottonwood crowd was slim—a piano player and her husband, the preacher and his wife, and a couple more couples. The love offering wouldn't have paid the gas bill for a trip past the end of the porch, much less to Alabama. But Daddy didn't do it for dollars. He knew his reward was waiting for him on the opposite bank of the Jordan.

Church regulars had the "slick road" excuse to miss the service. I'm sure the believers in the area hoped that when the final trumpet did blow, it wouldn't be during the rainy season. That way, God's gatherers could get back this far to collect them without getting stuck in the ditch. And if they are really lucky, the juke owner at the end of the road would have the neon light blinking so the angels would know where to turn.

There is one thing you can say about the South. You can throw a rock blindfolded and have about as good a chance of hitting a juke as you do a church.

Later on, when I started playing music in jukes, Daddy was still traveling and preaching. That made him and me more alike than folks might think, because that put both of us on the lookout for—and depending on—sinners.

I always figured this world contained about as many sinners as non-. That was why jukes and churches were open on different nights, one on Saturday and one on Sunday. That way the tonkers would have somewhere to go the next day where they could voice their regrets and ask for forgiveness—and get it—even if their shirt collars smelled like an Avon sample case and their breaths like mouthwash.

There was one talent Daddy had over me. He could deliver his fire and brimstone message with the same force whether the crowd numbered 1 or 100. I've always had trouble playing in an empty room. I still do. My enthusiasm is directly proportional to the number of ears listening—the more ears, the more enthused I was and am.

To me, it is disappointing to look out at empty tables. I figure it had to be just as disappointing for Daddy to look out at empty pews.

It's easy to be heartbroken and get hard-hearted over such disappointments. Broken hearts eventually heal for some people. But other people seem to have their broken hearts stitched back together with rusty barbed wire, sewn and resewn to a point where the combination of scars and sharp steel makes their hearts harder and harder to re-break. Not Daddy. The empty pews didn't seem to bother him, at least not on the outside where the barbed wire can't be seen.

But it had to, even if only on the inside—especially as many times as he dealt with it over the years.

Once he was the pastor of a community church in Kinard, Florida, where, on most Sundays, only one faithful man showed up for the service. And as Daddy thundered from the pulpit, the man had his head lowered, not praying, but dozing.

Then there was Page Pond Assembly of God, where he preached to empty pews for a week during an August dry spell. Unlike the people in Cottonwood, the no-shows didn't have a "slick-road" excuse. They had their own excuses—the church had no air conditioning and no screens on the open windows to keep the mosquitoes out.

For a short time, Daddy was also the pastor at a church in the one-store/one-church/no-juke joint community of Sumatra, Florida, where he went every Sunday.

If there had been a way to cut across the Big River swamps, Sumatra was only 12 miles from our house. But there was no such shortcut unless you could use alligators as a bridge and cottonmouth moccasins as shoes. So to get to church, he had to drive to Blountstown first, then to Bristol. From there he drove through the community of "Stiff and Ugly," on to Wilma and from there on to Sumatra—a 72 mile trip one way just to find empty pews.

So in my mind, he would have had plenty of excuses for his heart to harden. But it never did. No rusty old barbed wire ever found its way in.

But it did find its way to the hood of that '62 Chevy resting sideways in an Alabama ditch.

And all I can say is, thank God for sinners. Especially the one in overalls and wearing a straw halo; the one with a double load of tobacco and driving a Ford 9N tractor; the one with Listerine on his breath and Avon on his collar, because without such sinners, churches and jukes would be out of business. And we might still be in that Alabama ditch.

Surrounded By Preachers

TWO AGAINST ONE

"NEVER CAN TELL," I said to the bathroom mirror. "I might just get to talk to a girl tonight."

It was Saturday night, and I had a lot working in my favor—I was 16 and not all that ugly, if you didn't consider my looks. After all, I didn't have that many pimples, and I had permission to use the family Chevy. It had a radio that worked and could pick up the Panama City station. Plus, I had $2 in my pocket for gas. I made that wad of money counting worms for Mr. Capps. He was the owner of "The Sign of the Shiner" bait and tackle store at the foot of the bridge crossing the west arm of the Dead Lakes.

"Nope, never can tell," I said as I looked in the mirror and brushed my front teeth with my finger.

I filled the tub with water and took a bath, just in case. Then I drove into town, just in case.

But what happened in town that night during the mid-1960's is what always happened on Saturday nights in Wewahitchka, Florida. Half a dozen of us teenage boys would gather at a downtown lot, optimistic and smelling like Hai Karate.

There wasn't a girl in sight, just like all the other gatherings. "Dang," I said to the rearview mirror. "Another wasted bath!"

Standing on the dirt lot in a circle as we always did, we were under-washed and over-optimistic. There we waited and talked about the important things in our lives: dual pump carburetors as long as your arm and the best spark plug to use in an Evinrude. Sometimes we'd argue about which stink bait worked best to catch catfish or who won the drag race across the dam bridge last Sunday. And we always speculated about who it was that put the goat in the post office lobby that historic Halloween night.

And, of course, we talked about girls, only because they weren't there to defend themselves. They were somewhere else. We just couldn't figure out where.

If the truth be known, the girls not showing up was a good thing. They would have scared us half to death and stripped us of our ability to sound out our vowels.

Sometimes we'd also brag at a low volume about how we'd outsmarted the town's only policeman, Chief Jonathan "Preacher" Glass.

We'd outsmarted nobody, especially him.

Preacher Glass had the uncanny ability to know what we might do even before we knew what we might do. He was not a preacher in the biblical sense but did have his list of "shalt nots" he expected people to live by.

How could one man in one police car surround us just before we did what we thought we might do?

Preacher Glass was an icon in the community. He was as tough as a twice-fried pork chop off a Piney Wood Rooter. That's a wild and wiry hog that roamed nearby swamps and survived on palmetto roots, crawfish, and little boys who didn't mind their mamas. At least, that's what Mama told me when I was little. "If you don't straightin' up and fly right," she'd say, "I'm gonna throw you to the hawgs."

Rumors ricocheted around that Preacher Glass had been shot so many times that he had more lead in him than an average-size tackle box. They also said he was made a lawman because "the law" just couldn't do anything with him. I always heard that his wife once shot him off a motorcycle with a shotgun. It didn't kill him—just added to his tackle box.

It was told that one night a clench-fisted man accused Preacher of hiding behind his police garb, as if a short-sleeved cotton shirt with the sleeves rolled up made Preacher the man he was.

Legend says that Preacher stripped down to his boxer shorts, threw the man into the back of the squad car, and hauled him to the county jail. They said Preacher Glass was still half naked when they arrived.

Preacher gained hero status after a parent allegedly shot and wounded outside of a high school basketball game. I was there that night when Preacher had a young, unruly boy by the scruff and dragged him by me on their way to the door. That boy's father was later accused of ambushing and shooting Preacher in the right arm. After Preacher recovered, that arm stayed bent out at the elbow, as if he were Marshal Dillon about to draw his gun.

A picture of Preacher in a hospital bed, bandaged and grinning, was printed on the front page of a regional newspaper.

From that point on, it was almost as if the man could walk on water. At least it seemed he could while standing on the broad shoulders of the *Panama City News Herald*.

The talk of that reputation always fired the desire in us teenage boys to outsmart him.

Well, it turned out that he had a secret weapon for staying one step ahead of us. No, not a magic ring he got from a cereal box or a crystal ball that foretold our yet untold adventures. It was far less dramatic than that.

A network of "volunteer" spies is what he had—a small network made up of mamas and daddies. He knew them all, and they all knew him. Together, they all worked against us in tandem, or at least it seemed that way.

It's hard for boys to have a good time with so many watchful eyes squeezed into such a tight little place. Wewa was a town so small that if you got a running start, you could almost frog hop from one city limit sign to the other.

In a town that small, everybody knew everybody, so even before I was a Chevy-wielding teenager, my parents knew Preacher Glass and his daddy. Cecil Glass used to drive around the side streets and dirt roads in his old car. Wired to the top was an RCA speaker with gospel music distorting throughout the neighborhoods while Cecil called out the Wednesday specials at Revell's IGA.

When I was younger, Daddy would call Preacher from time to time after our neighbor fell off his donkey in front of our house and passed out in the middle of the road.

It was hard to tell which one had the most to drink, the man or the donkey. I guess it was a good thing our neighbor liked the sweet feelings the sour mash gave him. That way, when his head spun one way and the donkey the other, hitting the ground didn't hurt. At least not right away.

When alcohol breaks your fall, it postpones the pain until the next day. If you can't stay on your donkey and there's no 90 proof cushion between you and the dirt, it hurts twice as bad: both now and then—both that day and the next.

Mama is the one who pressured Daddy to call Preacher Glass. I doubt Daddy cared. But to her, it just didn't look right to have a sinner with corn squeezings on his breath passed out in the road in front of a preacher's house. Even if that road was dirt.

When Preacher Glass arrived, Mama made me go into the house so I wouldn't witness a live contradiction to every Sunday school lesson I ever had crammed down my gullet.

Mama didn't want me watching as it played out before my inexperienced eyes. But I sneaked out the back door and hid in the Elephant Ears and watched anyway.

Preacher pulled his police car up close to the limp body and blew the siren. He was hoping the man would jerk up his head and bump it on the bumper and think he was about to show up at Heaven's gate with a chrome dent in his head. That didn't work. Our neighbor didn't even grunt.

Preacher gathered him up like a wet dishrag, then delivered him around the corner to the man's house. There the wife was no doubt waiting to squeeze the squeezings out of her husband.

For various reasons, Preacher built relationships with many families in town. We boys didn't stand a chance.

Preacher turned out to be a lot smarter than a gaggle of teenage boys nesting on a parking lot thought he was.

A few of the boys thought Preacher might have been paranormal, because he knew more about what was going on than a pair of normal folks.

I thought that, too, because it was as if he could send Daddy a telepathic message saying, "All right, he's on his way home." That way Daddy could watch out the window to see if it took me more than one try to find the doorknob.

As I walked in the door, there he'd be, standing at the threshold, ready to sniff my breath and interrogate me as only a Holiness preacher could about what in the world could I find to do in Wewa on a Saturday night that kept me running the roads until 11 o'clock.

I'd shrug my shoulders and hold my breath. I never had the want to confess my sins. Besides, it's hard to say anything when you're not breathing.

There was no need to tell him my version of the truth, anyway. The city-appointed "Preacher" had already told the holiness preacher the authentic version.

What's a young sinner to do but shrug his shoulders when he finds himself surrounded by preachers of such marked contrast—one holding a Bible and one wearing a badge, one at home and the other one everywhere else.

Summer

SHORT PANTS, LONG DAYS

"YOU BETTER BE BACK here by dinnertime!"

Those were the last words I heard as the spring on the screen door stretched open and squeaked like a rat with a cat at each end.

"And don't slam that....!"

Too late! I'm sure all the squirrels jumped as the flimsy door banged shut behind me, sounding like a 410 shotgun during hunting season.

It was mid-May. The time of year when pants were getting shorter and days were getting longer. The 9-month sentence imposed on me by my parents and the Gulf County Florida Board of Education was being whittled down a little at a time by school days as long and dull as preachers who get paid by the hour.

Not Saturdays though. They were short and sharp. So sharp that they cut Saturdays down to half as long as a Monday, but twice the fun.

But school would soon be out for the summer. After that, the exploits would be daily, not just on Saturdays, and I'd be like a blind possum in a chicken coop—I wouldn't know where to start.

Half of those long summer days I'd fill with logging-road rambles and blackberry brambles.

"Don't you be late for dinner or I'll throw it to the dog," Mama hollered from the kitchen window as I loafered out of sight.

Daddy was already in the garden dusting the peas. He thought he was killing stink bugs. Chasing them over to Uncle Roy's garden was more like it. My brother was still asleep. That meant Mama had the house to herself.

Such moments were as rare as welcome mats at a funeral home, so it was cause for celebration. She could relax for a little while. To celebrate, she crumbled cornbread into a glass of cold buttermilk and sat on the porch swing.

Using standards set while she was growing up in Depression-riddled south Alabama, slurping a cornbread/buttermilk combo while sitting on the porch with dirty dishes still in the sink was close to being a sin.

But it was a Saturday. Besides, she had the house to herself, so nobody was looking. She figured even God had his head turned the other way, watching and laughing at Daddy herd those stink bugs.

To the dog's disappointment, I made it back home by dinnertime. Mama made sandwiches with fried bologna scorched around the edges, and no nap was required when I finished. Life was good.

The air was still thick with the smell of mustard and the sound of unheeded orders to not slam the screen door as I ran out again, this time to meet Saturday afternoon.

It was the un-scorched era between Korea and Vietnam—a time when words like "heat index" and the "stock market index" were as foreign to me as Indochina and New York City. It was a time when the only air conditioner was a can of Glade "Spring Flower Collection," sitting on the back of the commode; a time when red wasps lived under the eave and their stings were doctored with a wet snuff poultice fresh from somebody's bottom lip. Snuff spit was the all-purpose treatment used as an antidote to make the stings feel better. It seemed to work, too—as long as it was your mama doing the daubing.

The official school exodus had not even started and that screen door and I were already coming unhinged. Daddy would have to re-tighten the screws at least once during the summer, maybe twice if the clear outside days outnumbered the rainy inside ones.

It would be a year before my music career would arrive in a box from Sears. So there was no stage to be on, no request for "Wildwood Flower" or "Tom Dooley," just woods to romp.

I had this one day to myself and, like Mama, I needed to take advantage of it. Tomorrow would be Sunday, which meant church and most of the day already spoken for. After Sunday school we'd have to sit through an eternity sermon where a sweaty, screaming, long-winded preacher with fire in his eyes and Deuteronomy on his breath would try to scare the hell out of us boys. He was pretty good at it, too! I could have told him that a sermon half as long was twice as good, but he wouldn't have listened. Besides, that would have earned me a pinch from Mama and maybe a "whoopin" threat from Daddy. Smothering the pronunciation of that word in a south Alabama accent made it sound like a more severe punishment than a plain ole "whipping," and it was. Mama "whipped." Daddy "whooped." I can testify that there is a difference between the two.

After supper on Sunday, I'd play outside under the light of a Rural Electric Cooperative moon. It was always full, unless a thunderstorm shorted it with a limb or a squirrel suicided itself and shorted out a transformer.

Boys have changed little since that time. The adventures have, but not the boys. In those days before digital, the adventures mirrored the old ways washed down from Appalachia like a slow creek on its way south, swelling as it picked up trickles of adages along the way.

Because of those old ways, I spent days wondering if the rustle in the leaves might be that elusive coachwhip snake we'd all heard about. My cousins told me that the snake would grab his own tail and form a wheel out of his body, then run you down and "whoop" you when he caught up with you. I never saw this happen and my cousins never produced any lash marks as proof. But just like "his-and-her" cook pots on the devil's stove, you didn't have to see it to know that it's true. Especially if the one telling you knew how to tell it with flair and with a poker face.

As a cure for the after-effects of a frog peeing in your hand, we'd count how many warts we had and gather that many small rocks and put them in an old sock. After tying a knot in the end, we'd back up to a clump of bushes and throw the sock back over our right shoulder. Following the instructions handed down by our ancestors, we'd walked away without looking back. Our kin swore that ritual would cast off the warts.

We made sure all the dead snakes had their bellies pointed down and not up, because a belly pointed up was a good way to get your Saturday rained down on.

And if we saw a dead frog in the road, we'd draw a circle around it with a stick, lean over the circled corpse and spit'n'wish. If your spit landed inside the circle and hit the dead frog, that was a sure-fire way to make your wish come true. Our kin swore that this method doubled your chances when compared to making a wish and blowing out birthday candles. It just didn't taste as good.

We never questioned if these notions worked because our kin never questioned them. They just passed them on to us. They figured we might need them one day, like a sock full of extra rocks in a dresser drawer, lying around, waiting on a frog to pee on our hands.

It was all just a mystery. And we understood that some mysteries in this universe will never be understood, and were never meant to be—like why bologna just tastes better when it's fried. Or how a daub of anything applied to a wound by your mama would make the hurt go away.

Mail Order Guitar

DREAMING WITH YOUR EARS OPEN

"IF THEY SANG ONE more chorus of 'I'll Fly Away,' my fangers are gonna fall off." It was so loud in there, nobody could hear me complaining. I was just glad the preacher couldn't read lips.

The paradise they sang about was a long way from here. The paradise I was thinking of was more like a pair-a-dice in somebody's pocket down a short ways from the church in that cinder-block tavern filled with sinners and over-used cigarette smoke. That somebody was as loaded as the dice in his one pocket and the cheap pistol in his other.

At this moment in my life, I was not there playing my guitar. I was here playing it in church, just like I promised Daddy I would.

At least those ten choruses gave me the chance to sprout new wings and try out that new guitar lick I'd stolen from a Chet Atkins record I had borrowed from my uncle. It also gave me the opportunity to realize that I needed to practice that lick a lot more, along with callusing my fingertips more.

When the spirit was moving between the pews, nobody was paying attention to my guitar licks anyway. It wouldn't have mattered to them if I had come close to sounding like Chet's. They were listening to Jesus, not me. I figured the people inside the block tavern would be the opposite.

I'd been picking a guitar for only a few months, so the tips of the fingers on my left hand hurt like I'd been picking blackberries after dark.

Those Black Diamond strings sure didn't help. "I seen hog wire thinner than them thangs," I remember telling the guy behind the counter at the drugstore where I bought them.

"Take 'em or leave 'em," he said, confident that we would complete the deal and I'd hand over all the money I'd made that week cutting grass. After all, he owned the only place in town selling guitar strings.

Eight verses of "Some glad morning, I'll fly away...." were behind us and the singers hadn't even left the ground yet. The small congregation at the Assembly of God church showed no signs of running out of volume, enthusiasm, or wind beneath their wings.

Each chorus was like a slight turn of the gas knob on a stove. The flame was higher and hotter until the pot—or pews in this case—got too hot to touch and the Holy Ghost started walking amongst them. Then somebody would holler "Well Glory," and several of the choir members would start hopping around like they were the first people to do-si-do on the sun.

A couple of men seemed to be close to levitating as they jumped from pew to pew, leaping across children sleeping on pallets while their mamas danced in the choir.

Aunt Eunice had her face down on her knees, the top of her head bumping the back of the second pew. She was "speakin' in tongues," a melodic babble that was said to be coming straight from God. She'd look up now and then to see if anybody was listening.

Brother Deese was flat on his back on the floor, "slain in the spirit." That's where he'd been since the fifth chorus. With hands pointed toward the sky, he looked like a referee that Jesus had run over while crossing the goal line, scoring a touchdown against the Devil's team.

Brother Alf and I had our guitars cranked. Sister Daniels was bouncing so hard on the piano stool that the legs were wobbling as bad as the legs down the road at the honky tonk. She pounded those piano keys like she was killing serpents.

Early in my music career, those high-octane services are where I did all of my playing—because of that promise I'd made Daddy.

"I'm gonna git you that 'lectric git-tar and amp-per-far from the Spiegel catalog," he said months earlier. "But you'll have to play it in church and not in no honky tonk."

That promise I kept—well, with that guitar and amp anyway.

Besides, at that point I wasn't even old enough to get in a juke's front door. Maybe the back door, but not the front.

And I sure wasn't ready to get on stage with "The Country Gentlemen." The band was a melodic collection made up of a mechanic, a pulpwooder, a life insurance salesman and one guy between jobs. All of them had a knack for keeping the Hank flowing as long as the beer was. The stage was in a corner of Cherokee Tavern, a spot chosen only because it had an electrical outlet nearby.

Wewahitchka, Florida, had only one red light, but two juke joints. One was on the north side of town, the other heading south. That way, you could get quenched whether you were "a'comin' or a'goin'."

The juke Daddy was talking about was the one heading south, the one we could hear through the woods on Saturday nights.

It's surprising how far the sounds of sinning can travel. Even when it's having to cross one creek while dodging two miles of bay trees. The sounds of frenzy and frolic would end up coming uninvited through the bedroom window as I lay listening and dreaming with my eyes and ears open.

On weeknights to get my music fix, I listened to the radio. Daddy could make me turn off the radio. But on Saturday nights, he couldn't make "The Country Gentlemen" turn off their amps. And it was too hot to close my window and put glass between me and them. So all he could do was pray.

Mama tried to keep my nose pointed down the right road, but that dream kept getting in the way. To her, almost any road would've been okay as long as it was heading away from the source of that neon sound ricocheting through the woods.

Then one Sunday, the church drummer let it slip.

"The bartender at the Cherokee Tavern'll pay you cash to play that guitar down there." I don't think Mama ever forgave him for cracking the lid on that jar and letting the Devil escape.

"A lot of bad things go on in them places," Mama said. And if I took the wrong turn and ended up there, I would get in trouble with the Lord and maybe even with the law. She begged me to never take a bite of that forbidden fruit being sold inside that smoky stand along that wrong road. She told me it was a place where sin came in pop-top cans, and people fought while dark bottles flew through the smoky air like bats flying through a foggy night.

But you know what they say about forbidden fruit. It makes the best jelly. Especially to a boy with bright stage lights in his mind's eye, keeping him awake at night while he listens to music bounce through the swamps.

In my mind, I already had my blinker on to make the turn onto that road Mama had warned me about.

When I got old enough to buy a different guitar and amp not shackled by a promise, I plugged it into wall outlets south and north of town. And Mama and Daddy prayed I would get convicted by the Holy Ghost and not by a jury of my peers. Either that or maybe God would somehow see fit to break my E string.

To them, it sure looked like I was flying away, just like in the song, only I wasn't bound for "The Promised Land." They worried because to them it looked like I was headed straight for the county courthouse by way of the Cherokee Tavern and Dave's Bar.

The Hunting Trip

THE GRINNING SQUIRREL

BECAUSE OF THE DROUGHT, we could walk across the dry bottom of the river slough. Last spring we caught brim in that same spot.

I could see the high water mark across the cypress trunks. It was a dark to light transition line about the height of an average man. Well, one might have used that comparison if those swamps along the Chipola River Cutoff had ever produced an "average man." Finding such a person around those cypress knees would be as rare as finding a pulpwood truck that came with a CD player.

It was the day after Christmas. It was cold. Most December mornings in North Florida were cold. It was supposed to be.

The air was so crisp that it seemed fragile and in danger of shattering at the slightest thump by a limb. My red ears felt the same way. When I'd breathe in, the air tasted like a snow cone flavored with air.

Since Mama had laid out my clothes that morning, I had on three shirts, two pairs of pants and as many socks as I could pull on and still cram my feet into my boots.

I could barely move.

Daddy wore jeans. Not his town pair, but the faded ones that smelled like the paper mill. No matter how many times Mama washed them, they smelled that way. Hanging across his shoulder by a cotton strap was his homemade game bag. Mama made it from one of her old aprons that still had grease splatters on it. Dried squirrel blood stained the bottom of the bag, proof that Daddy knew how to aim a shotgun.

Daddy carried a 16-gauge shotgun he'd ordered from Sears. I carried a single-shot 410 he'd borrowed from the family's landlord, Mr. Mossy Cleckley.

The unbreeched gun lay across my shoulder like it was a drunk sailor and I was a bouncer. But unlike the sailor mentioned, the gun was unloaded. Daddy had promised Mama it would stay that way until we saw a squirrel.

This was my first hunting trip.—an unexpected Christmas gift from Daddy after he'd got an extra day off work because Christmas fell on a Friday that year.

"If we hear a squirrel, we'll sneak up on him while he's bark'n," Daddy said. "Cause when his mouth is talk'n fast, his ears are hear'n slow."

When Daddy was a boy during The Great Depression, they called grey squirrels "Hoover hogs," after President Herbert Hoover. They blamed the Depression on him. In Texas they called armadillos "Hoover hogs." I guess when you're hungry, it doesn't matter if you shoot them on the ground or out of a tree or if their tail has hair on it or not, they end up in the same place—in a "Hoover Hog" cook pot.

About that time, we heard a squirrel barking in the distance.

Inching in that direction, we chose the quietest places to put our feet as if we were both trying to sneak out of Sunday school class. "Gotta be as quiet as a cat sneaking up on a rat," Daddy said.

That was a pretty tall order for a boy with every pocket poked full of gun shells and one Barlow pocket knife mingling amongst them, plus a straightened coat hanger dangling from a belt loop like a scrawny saber, sometimes hanging by my side, sometimes tangled in my feet.

Despite all this clanging hush, the squirrel stayed put as we got into range. He was at the top limb of a Tupelo gum, sprawled out on a limb. Since we were able to walk up close, he must have been barking in his sleep. You know, like a dog does when he's asleep on the floor in front of the fireplace, dreaming about chasing a cat up a tree.

I don't know if my hand was shaking from the cold or from the anticipation, but I stuck it in my pocket and fumbled for just the right shell. It took two jerky tries to ring the barrel, but I loaded the gun, gripped the forearm sticky from the electrical tape holding it all together. Snapping the barrel shut, I pointed it toward the squirrel and pulled the trigger. A few leaves rained down as the blast echoed through the swamps, bouncing and ricocheting until it died.

But the leaves were all that fell out of the tree that day. The squirrel was still alive, still sprawled out on that limb, looking down at us. To me, he looked like he was grinning. I guess he knew a joke when he saw one, especially one wearing a dangling coat hanger.

"Reload," Daddy whispered as he kept the squirrel in sight.

"I'll give you sump'um to grin about," I mumbled as I unbreeched the gun, choked the tip of the barrel, tilted it toward me, drew the wire coat hanger and rammed it down the barrel's throat.

Mr. Mossy had told us to bring a coat hanger because the shell ejector didn't work and the spent shell casing would have to be poked out.

One good ram and the wire broke through. But all that hit the leaves was the brass end. The paper shell had swelled and clung to the inside of the gun barrel. So out came the Barlow and the hurried digging began.

While all this was going on, the squirrel got bored and left. So did we.

On the walk home, I carried the empty game bag, while Daddy carried both shotguns, including one with the paper shell still stuck in its throat.

It was going to be a long, disappointing walk home.

About halfway back, we stopped to rest, sitting on a log near a clump of saw palmettos.

For a long minute we sat in silence, me with my head lowered.

"I guess squirrels can have lucky days, too," Daddy said as he leaned sideways to fetch his knife out of his pocket. While seated on that log—me moping and him whittling—Daddy showed me how to make a whistle from a palmetto stem and a frond. He blew on it and it made a sound that turned a boy's frown upside down.

The whistles were easy to make. I made several and carried them home inside his game bag as the only trophies of the day.

Sixty years have passed, and I do not remember what I got for Christmas that year. But I remember that first hunting trip with Daddy and how to make a whistle from a palmetto limb.

That made it a good day, a lucky day for both boy and squirrel.

Step Up, Rodie

IT'S NOT GOD'S FAULT

DADDY HAD TWO BOOKS that guided him through life—the Bible to guide him in his day-to-day activities and the "Planters Almanac" to coach him in his dirt-to-dirt doings.

He was a farmer by blood who happened to be working at the paper mill to feed his family. But what was always deep in his heart was his affinity for digging holes and burying seeds. I guess as a preacher you could say he was still planting seeds in God's garden that he fertilized with prayer and faith.

As a compromise between farming, mill work and preaching, he settled for a small garden near the house.

I don't know if it's self-reliance, self-defense or self-satisfaction, but you can look behind almost all the houses in a working-class community and you will find a garden.

It doesn't take a lot of equipment to keep up such small plots. A hoe and a push plow will do it. A small tractor would also be nice. But, as a mill worker with a family to feed, Daddy couldn't afford a tractor, not even a small one.

But he knew where he could borrow a mule.

Rodie was a lanky critter with long, busy ears that telegraphed his every contempt.

The problem was, Rodie lived two miles away.

So on plow day we'd load up in our Chevy and go get him.

No, he didn't ride back to the garden plot in the backseat. I did.

I would hang my head out the backdoor window with a lead rope in my hand with Rodie hooked to the other end.

We'd creep along the road and Rodie would trot along beside the car, leaving behind a weak trail of dust mixed with oil smoke and a few fragrant slowdown bumps piled in the road. People following behind us had to be careful or else they might skid right on through a stop sign.

Along River Road we loped, the car's low gear singing with Rodie honking his horn. It was hard to tell if we were pulling a mule or if the mule was pushing us.

The car had a tendency to sputter now and then, but thank the Lord, it never backfired.

If it had, I'm sure Rodie would have bolted and I would've been sucked out the window and found myself mule skiing barefooted on a gravel road

At the garden Daddy hooked Rodie up to a plow that was leaning against a tree, waiting on them.

With ammonium nitrate spread between the corn rows, he'd throw the plow reins over one shoulder, cluck once, pop the reins and bark out his first order. "Step up, Rodie!"

The two would take off side-dressing the corn, leaving behind a dust cloud made up of North Florida dirt, a little fertilizer, a "WHOA, RODIE!!" or two, and what little religion Daddy might have brought with him.

This was before Daddy had been washed in the blood—a time when being washed in the sweat could force a man to talk mule language in tones that sounded like he was spitting out nails. It has always been hard to find a saint hanging onto the end of a mule's plow reins.

His temper would flare from time to time as Rodie seemed to forget his gee from his haw. It seemed he and Daddy had a different definition of "right" and "left." Daddy's mouth would curl up as if he were chewing castor oil-flavored gum and he couldn't get the taste out of his mouth, no matter how much he spit. I guess that's what mules taste like.

Either way, there was a lot of braying and not so much praying going on between those corn rows.

Daddy was not shy about announcing Rodie's maternal ancestry to those corn stalks.

Like many men of his generation, Daddy could speak a second language. As a survival skill back in Alabama, he had to learn by trial and error the language of "muleolgy." As a sharecropper he had to speak it every day to a wormy, flop eared, one-crop beast with nothing to lose by being cantankerous. With Daddy pushing and the mule pulling, they plowed up and down cotton rows that stretched to sunrise in one direction and sunset in the other.

The language that would shoot out from many an old farmer's mouth was like birdshot mixed with glass and vinegar blasting out the end of a 12-gauge shotgun. It would sting the ears of even the hardest sinner. Any mama within range would scoop up her child and rush him to the nearest church to have his ears flushed out with anointed water. If no anointed water was handy, just plain old Alabama water would do, as long as it came from a church spigot.

Meanwhile, Rodie continued to gee when he was told to haw and vice versa, as if he didn't understand a word hurling out of Daddy's mouth.

Mules are unique animals—somewhat like a cross between a Bible and a Planter's Almanac. But to a mule, the Bible he lives by would not see it as a sin to plant you in the ground. They are the offspring of a donkey and a horse. At some point back in history, somebody must have left a gate open after a horse and a donkey had too much to drink.

I read somewhere that a horse has 64 chromosomes, a donkey has 62, and their offspring, the mule, ended up with 63. So I guess it's understandable that an animal that has misplaced his horse chromosome might also misplace his gee and his haw.

Before you can understand a mule, you must first realize that God didn't create him. The mule is man's own invention.

And as humans, we sometimes want to place blame for some things on God when He had nothing to do with it. We are always looking for a scapegoat. So...

"Step up, Rodie."

Playing In Church

A SIGN FROM GOD

If you mix a little holiness music in with a better-than-average guitar picker, a drummer with Listerine on his breath, and a bass player with a shirt pocket full of promises to do better, you'll have yourself something worth shouting about.

The Sunday song service at a holiness church could sometimes be a gathering place for musicians caught somewhere between what preachers like Daddy described as the haints, the saints, and the hallelujahs.

Church is a place strummers and pickers, singers and liquor lickers are drawn to. There they can repent again and again and get back on God's good side after playing the night before down the road at the neon tabernacle. Could be, though, it's just the love of playing that draws them there. More likely, they figure a church is the last place a lawman with a warrant in his hand or an ex-girlfriend with a gun in her purse will show up looking for them. It doesn't matter what gets them to church. They are there, and I'm sure that's all that matters to God.

Sometimes it's other things that get them there, such as a malfunctioning sign hanging high on a lowly honky-tonk window.

Lucas Cain cut pulpwood during the week. On weekends he played music at the local juke where he seemed to always be thirsty, so his whiskey glass saw a lot more action than his tip jar.

He spent his days wrestling with a chainsaw. By looking at him, it was hard to tell who won. He was glad when Friday sundown showed up to relieve him. But by then, his arms ached, and he barely had the strength to hold up the bottle to the light so he could see if a quart of whiskey would still hold a gallon of demons.

"What do I do?" he asked his conscience. "Do I not drink and feel bad now, or do I drink now and feel bad tomorrow?"

It was a conundrum until he remembered that tomorrow was Saturday and he didn't have to work, so tomorrow won. Or did it lose? It's according to whether your view is from the top down or the bottom up.

With each swallow, his Adam's apple moved up and down like a kid bouncing a rubber ball on top of the septic tank lid while hoping it didn't all crumble.

In two days he would be up early again, the smell of gas fumes filling his lungs as he poured it into his chainsaw. After setting the can back down, he'd glance up to check the sky for rain, as if he could do anything about either—the gas fumes or the weather.

Stormy weather meant he could stay home. You can't cut pulpwood if it's storming—drizzling, yes, but not storming. It's too dangerous. As if staying home wasn't. You can't buy food for your family if you have too many stay-home days of freedom in a row. And if you drank a little whiskey, even if just on weekends, but didn't take care of your family, you were in danger, not of being cut or shot but worse—of being branded as "the sorriest thang God ever wrapped in hide."

He couldn't live with that tarnish on his name. Such shame would force him to look down at the floor when he met people in the bread aisle at the Piggly Wiggly. Especially the old folks who knew his daddy.

His daddy always said the only thing of value he had to pass on to his children was a good name. "So you better protect it even if you have to use both hands," he'd say. "It takes a lifetime to put your name up on a hill and only a drizzle to wash it all away."

Worrying about such things is a sobering thought. But as far as Lucas was concerned—on the weekend anyway—there was only one way to cure worry, and that was the same way you cured sobriety. And maybe while he's at it, forget about what caused the calluses and scars on his hands and his heart.

Lucas never drank on weekdays. Running a chainsaw and loading pulpwood is dangerous work. Who would feed his family if a stick of pulpwood fell on his head or a chainsaw developed a taste for flesh? He was their sole provider. If something happened to him, what would happen to them if all their eggs had to be put in one casket?

From the cradle on, life can be fatal. It has always been that way and always will. So you can't live worrying about dying. Doing that will put you in the ground before your designated planting time. If that happened, his family would have to depend on the bounty of the county just to eat. And as far as he was concerned, dependence on government handouts left little of a legacy his daddy would have bragged about if his daddy had still been on this side of Jordan.

Other than having to stoop and sweat a lot in the piney woods, his life hadn't been all that bad. At least he'd never had to be led away in handcuffs, or had to eat out of the government's trough, except for an occasional sandwich made from commodity peanut butter. But thinking back, it's easy to relive a good life when all you remember are the good parts.

It's easy to forget what loading pulpwood by hand can do to your back and what chainsaws can do to your knees, and what both can do to your dreams.

It's easy to forget what the cotton field and paper mill did to his daddy and why his daddy never talked about those sharp memories, but preferred to let them dull and rust like an axe sitting out in the rain.

But Monday would come soon enough, and the TV says there's no chance of rain so no worry about anything rusting, except for maybe the hinges on any door of opportunity.

Sometimes all he had left by Sunday was an empty bottle and hope that next week the mill wouldn't cut his wood quota. And hope that when he works himself to death and judgment day comes, that it comes on a Sunday. That way God won't be compelled to smell his breath before He lets him in the gate.

Well, Lucas didn't have to worry anymore about God wanting to smell his breath. This Sunday he was in church to play his guitar and tell a sober crowd about his experience the night before. Even if they didn't believe him.

It surprised people who knew Lucas to see and hear him playing in church on Sunday morning. His wife was especially surprised when that morning Lucas got up, wiped off his shoes with a damp washcloth and said, "I'm going to church with you this morning." She had been trying for years to get him to warm a church pew, even if it had to be one in the back row. But here he is today, standing in the front row with a guitar around his neck, testifying how the night before, while filling his glass again with sin, he saw a sign from God in that honky tonk window. To him, it was a message from on high that made him realize it was time to set things right with the Lord.

"I know y'all ain't gonna believe me," he said. "But I saw a glowing cross blinking in the winder at the juke around midnight last night."

Keen on seeing an opportunity to minister to the flock, the long-winded preacher interrupted him.

"Y'all don't hold it against a feller like this just because he used to play music in them places. Can I get'a amen? Some people say you cain't antagonize, analyze, scrutinize and evangelize all at the same time. I say you can and you should when a man like this is trying to body-slam the devil, and he wants us who's gathered today in God's arena to be his tag-team partner. Can I get'a amen? Many a professional sinner got his start in a honky tonk, where an Abraham Lincoln will buy you a shot of whiskey and a George Washington will buy you a jukebox chaser. Our new brother here has taken his world of haints and saints and traded hell in for the hallelujahs, and we should praise God for placing that glowing cross in that window last night. Can I get'a amen?"

Well, instead of thanking divine intervention, the preacher should have been thanking the rat that chewed the wires on that blinking "Falstaff" sign, causing all the letters except for the "t" to short out. God works in mysterious ways—sometimes even through rats.

"That cross in that winder got my Lucas in church today," his wife whispered to her pew neighbor. "And that's all that matters to me." Like so many honky tonk wives, Mrs. Cain hated the sin, but dearly loved her sinner.

In that church on Sunday mornings, all those Fender bending pew pickers looked as worn out as a pulpwood truck with only two payments left on it. But their hearts were in the right place. Or just down the road from it, anyway.

As a fledgling player. who'd just finished the last page in his "I'll Have You Playing Sharp In Nothing Flat" big-note guitar book, it was the music that I liked. It reminded me of the music we played when local musicians gathered and plugged in their amps at Boddye's Standard Oil station in Wewahitchka, Florida. It was music you could tap your toe to.

Holiness songs have spark to them. They have a beat and some of them are almost danceable—if you have a little imagination, any rhythm at all and the sky is clear with no chance of a lightning strike. Add to it a choir who had a tendency to sing "I'll Fly Away" for 20 minutes at a stretch, and it gave me plenty of opportunity to try out every page in that chord book.

The problem was—and probably still is—most of the songs they sang were in either the key of A*b*, B*b* or E*b*. Those are not good keys for guitar players. I guess whoever wrote the songs made them that way in case the devil's right-hand man picked a Fender or Gibson.

I contorted my fingers and played anyway. Daddy was on the front pew, telling ole brother so-in-so seated next to him, "I bought him his first guitar. I knew he'd go far. I just pray he don't end up in some old honky-tonk bar."

A capo would have come in handy for all those holiness anti-guitar keys.

The closest thing to a capo we had around our house was a pair of vice-grip pliers, and they were busy clamping the ground wire to the battery post in Daddy's Dodge. Besides, most of my musical cousins thought that depending on a capo made you weak, kinda like a glass of warm skim milk on a hot day instead of a sweaty glass of cold sweet tea. Country music star Little Jimmy Dickens said that you can throw a capo on the dash of your truck and it allowed you to park legally in a handicap zone. My cousins believed that, too.

I don't remember if it was the devil or the church drummer, but one of them said, "The girls'll think you're a cool cat if you'll learn to pick that guitar in nothing flat." At my age, the rhyming and the mental picture were all I needed to put me in high gear.

And what better place to learn than where the songs have a tank full of hi-test and the people dance on the pews?

A "Holy Roller" church is what the people in town called it. They meant it as an insult, but they were pretty well right. More than once, after a few courses of "Somebody Touched Me," I've seen them get happy, buck dance for a while, then drop to the floor and roll around. They looked like they were wearing yellow-jacket underwear and their haunches were hooked to a hot wire. Sometimes a dancing preacher would have to watch his step just to keep from stomping on a hallelujah.

This spectacle was nothing new for a few of the church musicians, and one day wouldn't be a spectacle for me either. After all, a holiness song service can sometimes look a little like a dance hall brawl, except without the cussing and spilled beer

Can I get'a amen?

Whole-Soul-Saver

WEARING HOLES IN YOUR SHOES

HE SET UP A small, used circus tent in a pasture not far from our house.

Every night for a week, he screamed into a microphone about how God loved His people and so did he.

Then, in the middle of the night, he left town in a hurry—tent, offerings and all—with another man's wife.

I don't remember his name, this Brother So-In-So.

All I remember is he danced around like his pants were full of ants, juggling four collection plates at once.

I couldn't figure out where in Wewa he found all those folding chairs.

Somebody put a lot of effort into getting them in such straight lines and spaced just right so a believer could reach back and get out his wallet without bumping the person next to him.

He was the first burning bushwhacker hiding behind a Bible that I remember seeing. I've seen plenty of them since then. You know, the kind who has a folding card table set up at the back of the tent, hawking autographed pictures of Jesus and other collectibles as you walk out.

If I sound cynical, well, I guess I am, at least as far as he and other charlatans are concerned.

Mainly because during that time Daddy was the only other preacher I really knew, the only one I knew to compare this one and others with.

So I knew, even at my young age, that this guy, who gladly took your money in exchange for telling you how to butter your own biscuit, could not stand the muster when standing shoulder to shoulder with Brother Woodrow Blackman.

For years I watched Daddy get up early on "The Day Of Rest," after working at that paper mill all week, and drive that white Chevy Bel Air eighty miles one way to Sumatra, Florida, to preach to two people, simply because it was the Lord's work. And when doing His work, miles, head count and quarters really didn't count.

Of course, that was twice the size of the congregation most Sundays when he preached at the

Kinard Community Church, a pulpwooding community twelve miles northeast of Wewahitchka.

I guess after pulpwooding all week, people there were just too tired to sin, so there was no need to go to church.

I remember many Sundays when, besides us, there was only one other person there.

And that one saint somehow managed to doze through the storm as Daddy thundered from the pulpit and ricocheted rounds of scriptures off the walls like lightning bouncing off a water tower.

I figured one of those bolts must have bounced off that man now and then because he would grunt, wipe his mouth with his handkerchief, then go back to dozing.

As a child, I was at both places, Sumatra and Kinard.

I can't tell you how many miles we rode in that car going to not only those churches but also attending Camp Meetings at Brother Hunt's in Panama City, Florida, and revivals at Brother Snellgrove's church in Midland City, Alabama.

And I can't tell you how many miles Daddy covered scooting his feet across the church floor, hurling "The Word" like rocks throughout various church buildings. Sinners either had to duck, flee, or take the lumps.

"The Bible says the Word will light my path and be a light unto my feet," Daddy preached. "I think that light unto my feet is a candle cause I can feel my feet warming up now." Then he'd start scraping across the floor like he'd just walked out of a chicken yard. "My feeeet are get'n hot. WELL GLORY!"

You could almost smell his soles heating up.

By now, the congregation was cheering him on like he just kicked the winning field goal, and the Devil was the football.

"WELL GLORY!" he'd shout again as he turned around and scooted back in the other direction, back and forth, up and down the aisle.

"THE WORD OF GOD HAS SET MY FEET ON FIRE!" His volume went up as he jumped up onto an empty pew, ran down it to the other end and jumped back on the floor. Then he'd shuffle back up to the pulpit as he shouted.,"I FEEL LIKE THE FIRST MAN WALKING ON THE SUN, ONLY I'M WALKING WITH THE SON. AND THAT SON IS JEEESUS! JEEESUS! JEEEEEEESUS! CAN I GET'A AMEN?"

By now, most everyone in the crowd was standing, hand-clapping and shouting in unison, "AMEN!"

Homilies in harmony with the Word were rough on his shoes. He took more than one pair to Mr. Brown's Shoe Shop to have them half-soled because of holes worn in the bottoms. I guess on a paper mill's take-home pay, a full-sole was out of the question, even for a whole soul-saver like Daddy.

For an entire childhood, my brother and I sat on wooden pews made sturdier by the dried chewing gum stuck under the bottom. We watched and listened as Daddy thumped his Bible and couldn't be still because God excited him, and Mama thumped our heads when we couldn't be still because it all bored us.

But I remember.

And to this very day, when I meet other preachers, I remember and I compare them to Daddy.

And only a few, a very few, can pass the muster.

A group of local ministers assembled inside a small community church for a monthly "meet and greet." It was an icy day as they gathered around the wood stove to fellowship with one another. Then the tramp showed up.

COLD AS HELL

A tramp, after spending a cold, wet night outside;

Went into a church where a crowd gathered with pride.

All were tightly wrapped around one glowing wood stove;

Waiting to start service inside, out of the cold.

The tramp stood in a lonely corner shivering;

And at the stove preachers stood, not one quivering.

None offering to share a warm spot with this man;

Not one volunteered, not one extended a hand.

So the tramp weaved toward the stove, first gee and then haw;

But never close enough he got so he could thaw.

"It must be cold outside!" one preacher smugly spoke.

"Cold as hell," the tramp said. His answer made them all choke!

"Pardon me," another preacher said. "But you are mistaken—

My Bible states that in hell sinners will be a'bake'n."

"No sir, it will be cold there," the tramp insisted.

"How do you figure that?" a third preacher persisted.

"It's simple," said the tramp in his tattered attire.

"There'll be so many preachers in hell that.......

A feller won't be able to get near the fire."

-Billy Blackman

Three Sisters

SEWING QUILTS

THE WIND SCATTERED THE cotton clouds across that summer sky. It looked like a dog had been playing with God's pillow and the frolic just got out of hand.

"Git in the car," Mama said. "We head'n down to your Aunt Mazie's house."

The air, sauteed in August with a splash of mosquitos, was too thin to breathe and too thick to ignore. It stuck to you like a car salesman after finding out you have a job and a little cash to pay down.

Folded up on the backseat was a quilt top. Mama's mama had cut out and stitched it together decades ago. What a tedious job that was for Granny Martin—cutting the small squares and diamonds from old shirts and feed sacks, sewing them together one-by-one, stitch-by-stitch, thimble pushing and fingers pulling.

In my mind, I can see her now.

There is no telling how many yellow cans of Dental Sweet snuff she went through getting that job done.

Lord only knows how much she loved her snuff. Grandpa loved his snuff, too. If I remember right, he dipped Railroad brand, which only goes to show you that people can live together without agreeing on every little thing.

She gave the quilt top to Mama and now it was on its way to Aunt Mazie's house to become a quilt that could warm you in more ways than one.

When we got there, the doors and windows on the almost-paid-for Jim Walter house were all open. It was more of a gesture of defiance against the North Florida summer than any relief it might bring on this windless day. On days like this, the air was so still that the leaves looked like a drawing on a sweaty artist's melting canvas.

Inside, three women would spend several afternoons sitting around a squared wooden frame that Daddy built. It was held together on each corner by wood clamps and suspended off the floor by small ropes tied to hooks screwed into the ceiling. The women, all sitting in straight-back chairs, looked different but similar, having obvious features from kindred stock.

From the oldest on down, they were three of the five Martin sisters. They were bound by common blood from uncommon ancestors as durable as the pine plank floors of their old homeplace that sat on the Alabama dirt many years ago.

Aunt Mazie—the oldest and the one who looked most like their mama, Aunt Eunice—next to the oldest, and Mama—the one born in the middle. Each sister was armed with a thimble, thread, and a needle. They sat side-by-side, looking out across colorful squares and diamonds Granny had cut from old work shirts, denim overalls and Purina feed sacks.

Sprawled in front of them like cotton rows of color lay days and days of work to be done. Rolled up in their wake were days and days of work already done. And sometimes, like another layer of icing on an already wonderful cake, Granny Martin would be there sewing too—sometimes in flesh, always in spirit.

Aunt Mazie was still raising a family in that Jim Walter house, and Mama was still raising a family in her Jim Walter house two miles away. Aunt Eunice had no children, but kept herself busy by tattling on dozens of nieces and nephews.

As a young boy still wearing yesterday's dirt, I was suspended somewhere in time between "Hey Diddle Diddle" and the ladies' bra section of the Sears catalog.

I would crawl up under the dangling frame and lie on the floor. From that vantage I'd look up and watch the sisters poking needle holes in the ceiling of my fort, stitching cotton clouds to the underside.

Under there, like a new lawnmower, my imagination would start on the first pull. Under there and in my mind I was whomever and wherever I wanted to be—from Captain Kangaroo to Winnie the Pooh, then Lash LaRue and Hoppy too. It was a boyhood fantasy, a who's who of Saturday morning TV.

I don't remember what the sisters talked about. It could have been about ole brother So-and-So selling buggy peas and okra so hard, that in a boy's imagination, he could use it to kill vampires. Or maybe they were taking turns testifying and quoting scriptures or nodding in agreement that Mr. Cicero Hoover at Revel's IGA was the best meat cutter in North Florida.

Beneath that canopy of cotton and color, I'd stay until the end of the day. Then, before dark, the chairs would scoot and bump back across the wooden floor. The sisters would stand and pull the ropes so the frame would rise until it was close to the ceiling. Then they'd tie it off, up and out of the way, so the living room, which was not much bigger than the quilting frame, could resume its original duties, its role in life.

Before I would crawl out, I would look up and see a sky that was now a patch of solid white cotton batting. It was as if the sisters, at least while inside that Jim Walter house, had the power and thread to stitch back together what that dog had torn apart in the real sky outside.

Up there above us all, the frame would hang until the next day.

"Git in the car," Mama said. "We go'n home 'cause your daddy'll be there directly."

That was fine with me because that elusive ice cream truck might just roll by the house that afternoon. I didn't want to miss chasing it with a little cold cash burning a hole in the pocket of my short pants. A dime could do that, you know.

The next day we'd go back. The sisters would lower the frame and take up where they'd left off. I'd crawl back into my fort so my imagination could take up where it left off.

These sisters were no longer young, but not old either. Over time, I would go to all three funerals, and I would sit on a pew and cry like a child after Father Time had demolished his fort.

Sometimes something will arouse those sleeping memories, blinking them awake the same way a barking fox wakes a sleeping dog in the middle of an unsettled night. And I will think about time spent under that quilting frame.

Everything just sort of fell into place under there. You know, kind of like when your Mama gave you a dime, and you'd chase the ice cream truck on foot with your pocket on fire. And then, right before you gave up, everything would get okay, because through the dust that tasted like vanilla and Ford exhaust, you'd see the truck's brake lights blink on.

Candy And A Claw Hammer

FROM THE INSIDE OUT

DADDY'S TREATMENT FOR A boy's cough included a piece of candy, a piece of cloth, and a whack from a claw hammer.

For doctoring shallow congestion, throat tickles, and minor coughing, he believed peppermint candy had healing powers.

The candy cane was the size of a small boy's wrist. He never said where he got it. I assumed it was part of his yearly safety bonus from the paper mill, like the $2 bills the mill bosses handed out when workers went all year without getting a finger cut off or a life cut short.

After breaking off a chunk of candy, he'd wrap it in a white handkerchief and give it a quick whack with his claw hammer. He looked like he was putting a ghost out of its misery.

The impact caused small pieces of peppermint to break off inside the handkerchief. The smaller pieces were just the right size for a small boy's medical treatment. A whiff of that handkerchief reminded me of Santa Claus.

To me, his doctoring method was much better than the one used by Dr. Canning, the doctor/mayor and sometimes veterinarian in Wewahitchka. His office was where riverboat captain Poley McDaniel's general store used to be.

The medicine Dr. Canning mixed came from the back room and smelled and tasted like he compounded it from equal parts of river mud, chicken toenails, and kerosene.

And to think, my parents paid him for it.

Mama had faith in Dr. Canning, but she also felt the need to add her own cure-all to his cure-all. Between the two of them and their doctoring, my tongue tasted like what the floor mat out of a dogcatcher's truck must have tasted like.

No, it wasn't snuff. It's a wonder it wasn't. Being from south Alabama, Mama would have dabbed a little snuff on a rattlesnake bite before covering it in prayer.

What she used to augment and improve Dr. Canning's medicine was a tablespoon of a colossal, cramp-causing concoction called Syrup Of Black Draught.

A bottle of it sat on a shelf in the kitchen, next to its cousin, the drain cleaner.

One tablespoon of Black Draught at bedtime and by midnight your stomach was sputtering like a Wizard boat motor with water in its gas. By the next morning your insides were as clean as a stump-slung chitlin.

That stuff was an overachiever when it came to doing its job. It was Mama's go-to remedy for everything from coughing to boys not wanting to go to school.

Veterinarians used to prescribe an early, home-made version of it for constipated cows and horses. Mama used the weaker store-bought human version. Well, it was supposed to be weaker.

After grabbing the black bottle off the shelf, she'd give it a shake. As I watched and dreaded, my eyes could not have been wider if she'd been shaking a black snake, a Bible, or a belt.

I don't know if between them—Mama and Dr. Canning—whether they actually killed any germs or just chased them out the back door.

Either way, it left me with a flushed look. But I felt better the next day. Or at least I said I did.

I walked out the door without coughing and headed to school. I was glad to go, and I didn't dare cough.

Many years ago, a young Dolly Parton did a commercial for Black Draught. "Black Draught makes you smile from the inside out," she said without coughing.

The only time it made me smile was after whatever ounce of it was inside my stomach was finally out.

Dolly's song made me miss Daddy and his claw hammer.

Get'n Happy

DUNKIN' AT THE LAKE

IF I HAD PUT my ear to the water and listened, bet I could have heard the word "H-A-L-L-E-L-U-J-A-H" sounded out one letter at a time as the bubbles popped at the surface.

But with so much rejoicing and speaking in tongues going on, it was hard to hear anything else, except maybe one of the Tyndall Air Base jets flying low overhead, practicing for that Vietnam war over there in places I couldn't pronounce.

John, Charles and I were still young. The Vietnam War was not on our minds as we waited and waded in the water. But it was the first thing on our parents' minds as they watched their boys come of age.

It was a cloudless morning. A good day for a baptizin'. No chance of rain. These folks knew what they were doing. They planned this event for the morning time, before the afternoon thunder started rumbling to the south. If they got wet today, it would be from the bottom up, not the top down.

Some folks believe in prayer only when the weather is stormy. These folks believed in prayer on the clear days, too.

The church crowd gathered around on the banks of Lake Alice, one of the twin-sister lakes that Wewahitchka, Florida, got its name from. Lake Julia is the other one. For local native Americans, the word Wewahitchka meant "water eyes."

Most who gathered at Lake Alice today were full-fledged "foot washers," while a few, like me and my friends, were full-fledged gawkers.

About a dozen grownups lined up in knee-deep water, waiting their turn to be led out where it was deeper to have their sins washed away. A couple of them smelled like the "catch'um end" of a crawfish drag. Maybe they had their weekly wash in mind. But who am I to judge? Sniff not lest ye be sniffed. I think that's in the Bible somewhere. But what do I know? I'm as close to being a Bible scholar as a water hose is to a water moccasin.

A small crowd of worshipers gathered to watch from the banks. A few watched from the children's park fifty feet away. The city built swings, slides and a merry-go-round on the shoreline. Kids gathered there to play. As teenage boys, we were there for a different reason.

We waded out and stood close to the preacher. It was shoulder-deep to us, but waist-deep to the grownups. We weren't there for religious reasons.

We had women's fashion and church doctrine on our minds.

The holiness faith frowned at the thought of women wearing pants, not even when they were in the pea patch or getting baptized in Lake Alice. Through biblical interpretation, women were required to wear dresses.

"And ya know," Charles said, as we were planning it all. "Sometimes the bottom of them there dresses will float to the top." Charles was the oldest and familiar with worldly things.

John was nervous about the future of our eternal souls if we pulled this off.

"Y'all think hell has a back door?"

"It does," Charles said, as if he knew it for a fact. "But they don't keep it locked."

John was relieved by that revelation. I was, too.

Our imaginations told us that the view would be like a real-time lingerie page from a soggy Sears catalog. As a bonus, we'd be under the murky water so our mamas couldn't see what we were doing. But John was still unsure.

"Y'all think God can see underwater?"

"Naw," said Charles. "Not without goggles on. And I never seed a picture of Him wearing goggles, have you?"

"I guess not."

We waited and practiced, taking deep breaths, holding it in for ever how long we thought it might take, then blowing it out. We were careful to remember to practice with our mouths shut. That lake water smelled and tasted a lot like tadpole tea.

Our Sunday School teacher was first in line. “Ooooh yea,” we thought in unison as we looked at each other. Charles winked at us both.

The preacher put his hand behind the sister’s neck and cupped his other hand over her nose and mouth. Then, shouting and churning the water with his happy feet, he preached to those waiting in line and those watching from the high ground.

“You ‘bout as well go out and get yoself a can of stop leak and a mop cause God done punched a hole in yo sinful heart and the Devil will be spill’n out all over the ground when you get back to dry land.” The dunking helpers near the preacher began shouting and stomping their feet, too. I saw a school of minnows scooting out to deeper water. Atheist, no doubt.

The hair bun on top of the sister’s head disappeared as the preacher pushed her under. He looked like he was dunking a Clairol-colored doughnut into a cup of watered-down coffee. With our mouths shut and our eyes open, we sank under with her.

We were ready for our prayers to be answered.

I guess God hadn’t been listening none of the time. We saw nothing! The water was too muddy. The holy roller buck dancers had stirred the bottom with their stomping around like they were trying to stomp out a magic fire that could burn under water. It was like looking through a bowl of chocolate pudding, trying to spot the spoon you dropped.

The sister came up. Her hem went down. She wiped the water out of her eyes and started shouting and dancing her way back to dry ground. "My sins have been washed away," she announced. We didn't know if it was the spirit making her dance or if a crawfish hitched a ride on her foot. Whatever the reason, she was stirring up more mud.

"Come on," Charles said. "We ain't gonna be able to see nut'n. Let's go up to the park."

From the park swings, we watched as the people continued dancing in the water, stirring up the mud. It was both entertaining and disappointing to watch. The disappointing part was we had to contrive a believable lie to tell our friends. Something had to be made out of nothing. The entertaining part was watching the more porky parishioners getting their sins washed away.

For these larger baptizees, the full dunk was a two-man job.

The preacher pushed on their foreheads to get them started under. His other hand held the back of their heads. A deacon was in the back to help hold up the more roly-poly holy folks so they wouldn't sink to the bottom if the preacher lost his grip.

Extra help is always handy if the baptizee starts wiggling in the spirit, slips and goes down on his own, maybe taking the preacher with him. That happened before and the churning water reminded me of when Tarzan was wrestling with an alligator, except the preacher didn't have a knife clinched between his teeth. But I admit, as he went under the water, the preacher's yell sounded a little like Tarzan's.

Most times it was a routine baptizing where the preacher-deacon team pulled the former sinner back to the surface, he or she bubbling on the way up. "H-A-L-L-E-L-U-J-A-H." You could hear those bubbles talking.

This "getting into the spirit" happened a lot. They called it "get'n happy," and once started, it would spread like chatter in a chicken house.

It involved a lot of motion and even more emotion, running in place and sometimes just running period.

The decibels would echo back and forth across the lake, making the event sound louder with every trip.

Then, between the hoedowns and hallelujahs, a song broke out. Everyone knew the words, so it spread like the spontaneous combustion from a pile of gassy rags.

"Yes, we'll gather at the river; The beautiful, the beautiful river." But they were not at a river. They were at a lake. That didn't matter. Like socks for Christmas, it's the thought.

Brother So-In-So would start shouting and running in place near the bank in the shallows, splattering joy on people's shoes and washing water bugs up onto the hill and onto Sister Eunice's legs. That would start her shouting and the chain reaction of emotion would spread like a bunch of hornets looking for whoever tore down their nest. And soon, everybody would be jumping around, swatting at the Devil.

Sister So-In-So would start shaking her head. The bobby pins started letting go and hitting the water like skeeter hawks diving after wiggle tails.

From where we were swinging, it looked like they were all walking on water.

"Ya know, they say Jesus could walk on water," John said.

"Ah, that ain't nut'n!" Charles said. "I seed skeeters a'walk'n on water a'plenty a'times."

We waited for the stomping to slow down so the mud could settle. We could try it again and, if successful, not have to lie about it. By not having to lie, we were safe since God didn't include gawking on his list of thou shalt nots.

But there was too much "get'n happy" going on for a chance at a second chance.

"I wonder where the preacher learned to baptize people?" John asked as he drug his feet to stop his swinging.

"It's in a book at the church," Charles said. "I seed it."

"What did it say?" I asked.

"The preacher is supposed to hold you under 10 seconds fer every sin you committed or even thought about committing that week."

"Ten seconds for each sin?" I said. "Well, in that case, I'll never have my sins washed away. I cain't hold my breath that long."

That Beacon On The Hill

BACON AND BEANS

IT'S FUNNY HOW A smell can trigger a memory. Sometimes it can be the other way around. We would ride south in that almost new, white '62 Chevy—Daddy driving and Mama directing, my brother, our Alabama cousin and I in the back seat. Our bare legs would squeak across the seats like we were sitting on mice as we bounced across the barge at Overstreet. The government made the floating bridge out of an old barge so people could drive across the Intracoastal Waterway.

Whenever boats needed to pass, the bridge tender would start a diesel engine and winch the barge out of the way. Once the boat passed, he'd winch it back into place. Then the white Chevy's with back seats full of noisy nimrods wearing arm floaties could continue south, toward that rich banquet of sounds, seagulls, sand crabs and sea oats. I could smell the briny aroma before I could see it. Taste it, too. It had a clean, tangy smack to it, different from the way the air tasted just 20 miles inland where we lived. There the air tasted like catfish and Uncle Roy's Camel smoke. And the salt air tasted nothing like the air a hundred miles north where our cousin lived. The air there tasted like cotton dust and peach cobbler. My mind can still smell the beach air if I think about it. It reminds me of the smell of a salt shaker as it anoints a grouper sandwich. Such a meal is a bounty from Gulf County. Especially when it's resting on a shallow pile of barbeque chips, and a'do-si-do-ing around a Coke chaser in a sweaty glass bottle. That beach smell always makes me hungry. The thought of it still does. My folks would save money all year so they could rent a beach house for three days at Beacon Hill, near Mexico Beach. From the early 1800s, the lighthouse there helped sailors find their way into St. Joseph Bay and the deep waters of Port St. Joe harbor. By the time we started staying in the house close by, the lighthouse had been moved and replaced by a simple flashing light adorning a metal tower. The rental house belonged to our former landlord. It sat about 100 feet from the beacon tower that gave the community its name.

Like Mama and Daddy, I had a little money in my pocket too. I saved it from my worm-counting pay

I got at "The Sign of the Shiner," a bait and tackle store on the banks of the Dead Lakes.

Yes, I was the worm counter there. My primary job was taking lard cans containing 1500 wigglers, earth and red worms collected by the "grunters" and dividing the contents into 50 and 100 count piles. Then I'd put the piles into cardboard containers to sell. I stacked them on shelves in the store next to the pickled eggs and potted meat. If you were going fishing that day, you needed this holy trinity. It was like the adage about the chain gang and the rock pile where you made "lit'uns out'a big'uns." Here, though, I made little containers of worms from a big container.

These "grunters" went to the woods every day equipped with the tools of their trade: a wooden stob, a flat piece of iron, lard cans and a love of autonomy. They sought cleaner places in the woods where a wildfire had burned the underbrush away. Such clearings were smutty and black on the top, but rich underneath in what they sought.

And if they couldn't find a clean spot, rumor was they'd take a match and create one. In doing that, they sometimes ran sideways with the law. Of course, that was just a rumor.

They'd find a good spot and hammer the stob into the ground.

Then, dropping to their knees, they began rubbing the flat iron back and forth across the top of the stob. They played it like a laid out bass fiddle after having too much to drink. Back and forth, they pulled and pushed their iron bow to the tempo of that fiddle classic, "The Arkansas Traveler."

But the music they created sounded more like a hog grunting than it did any fiddle song. On still mornings, especially if the fog was thick and the same color as a dingy ghost outfit, the grunting sound could haunt the airwaves a half mile away. That ghostly reverberation could cause a skittish person to go inside the house and wipe the dust off the Bible.

This collaboration of flesh, iron, and wood created a vibration that rooted through the ground. And before you knew it, just like a dance floor during a fiddle song, the ground came alive, not with buck dancers or two-steppers, but with fish bait.

The sight of these "worm charmers" busy at work would make most cynics believe in magic.

After the worms were charmed to the surface came the stooping and gathering, putting the worms into lard cans and delivering them to area bait houses.

One point of sale was "The Sign of the Shiner" where I worked for Mr. Capps every Saturday for $1.25 an hour. That was big money for a 12-year-old in the 1960s.

I remember the "charmers." They were giddy and gritty and smelled like independence. Their clothes raveled, their life revered and always in good humor. Most Saturdays they'd deliver two or three lard cans, sometimes more if the river level was high, which meant backwater fishing was good. That river stage would likely draw extra anglers from Panama City in search of bait and beer and other fishing requirements, like pickled eggs and potted meat.

Worm counting would not be found on a list of glamorous jobs. That didn't matter to me. I was glad to have the work. It paid an honest day's wage for an honest day's work—the mantra of the working class.

Plenty of times Daddy had said contentment was about what you did with your heart, not your hands. He was right. To him it didn't matter if you were stooped over putting worms in a can, stooped over taking worms out of a can, or stooped over a banker's desk counting your profits, your heart needed to be in a grateful state of mind.

But in the public eye, unless you were a grave digger, you couldn't get much lower in the social pecking order than picking up worms for a living. Or in my case, counting out worms into piles and making lit'uns out'a big'uns.

But despite what society folks thought then or think now, I believed worm charming qualifies as a higher calling. It also enabled me to have a few dollars in my pocket as we set out for the beach.

Even now, the smell of dirt makes me think of the worm grunters just like the ocean smell makes me think of Beacon Hill.

For three days at that beach house, we spent daylight hours in the salt water and nighttime hours on the porch listening. The drowsy night sounds of flopping waves whispering in our ears never changed cadence. They were like nature's metronome set to the warm rhythm of the last slow song of the night. That pulse was in sync with the blinking beacon reflecting off the porch floor that looked like bolts of lightning flashing from a far away storm with nothing to say.

I had never experienced a wave big enough to knock me down. Until then, the most impressive wave I'd seen was the wake of Durden Hall's bateau as he passed by on his way up the Chipola Cutoff to check catfish baskets.

All his waves did was give your cork an extra bobble and for a few seconds made it harder to tell if you were getting a bite.

I found out the Gulf of Mexico waves were big enough to knock me over and pull my baggy swimsuit down to my knees.

If I stood on the beach—after I pulled my swimsuit up—and looked east around a long hazy shoreline curve, I could see the paper mill smokestacks in the distance. They stuck up like beacons with their bulbs blown from a short in the wire that caused them to smoke. For decades those brick beacons guided Alabama cotton croppers like Daddy to the safer waters of steady paychecks, life insurance, paid vacations, and a pension plan.

Some people would complain about the mill's smell. "Smells good to me," Daddy said. "Smells like beans and biscuits a'cook'n." Later, along with a lot of other men, he found out that while the prosperity tasted and smelled good, in the end it ate up your lungs.

The mill is now gone—just a ghost in the minds of a few old timers. Sometimes on foggy nights when the wind and their minds are just right, those who remember will whisper that they can still smell those "beans and biscuits." But nobody ever says it out loud. If they did, a preacher or a policeman might want to smell their breaths.

Sometimes during those three days we'd go into St. Joe to buy groceries and to predict the weather.

If a south breeze was blowing the mill smoke through town and the smell was strong along Reid Avenue, it was a sure bet rain was coming. Most times it did.

In town, Mama would buy her Roman Meal "diet" bread cut into thinner slices to cut the calorie count. I think it did more for her conscience than it did her waistline. For us, she'd buy a loaf of regular bread and a pack of hotdogs and bologna. A folded over slice of that regular bread would serve as our hotdog bun.

I have always wondered what it was about that beach house that made the taste of bologna sandwiches and hotdogs so memorable. Was it that there was sometimes a little sand in our wiches and our britches? Don't know. But the memory of it will still cause me to smack my lips.

I think the salty air on our tongues made the bologna taste like round steak.

Even though we sometimes sat on the sand in folding chairs with goggles over our eyes, ate pork rinds and smelled like coconut suntan lotion, we didn't consider ourselves tourist.

Out there, we mingled with our people. They could have all been our kin. It was a working-class beach.

Men who yesterday rode tractors in Georgia or Alabama were today walking around in flip-flops and cut-off work pants with snuff-tin tattoos on the back pockets. Their arms were burned clay-road red from working in the sun and their legs were whiter than the beach sand their kids were using to build castles. They smelled like Old Spice and diesel fuel.

If you took a picture, it would look like the cover of the swimsuit edition of "Progressive Farmer" magazine.

Smelling like coconuts and mustard, with blue dolphin floaties around their chests, gullets full of salt water and swimsuits full of sand, their kids played and baked in the sun, summer after summer. Once grown, their kids took their kids and did the same, summer after summer, generation after generation. They did this because there was something that special about this place.

Still is.

But it's changing.

After Hurricane Michael washed it all out to sea, coastal counties enacted stricter building codes. Under those new guidelines, some families didn't have the money to rebuild. Rich folks and big corporations did.

It all feels different now.

But no matter who rebuilds it or how it's done, there will always be something special about the memories. They are like a flashing beacon, directing my childhood reveries to safe harbor.

I remember how it smelled, how it tasted, and what it looked like, even without Daddy's "beans and biscuits" to remind me.

Buttermilk And Whatnots

MYRRH, CALAMUS, CINNAMON

My family thought a quick sip of buttermilk and a slow walk to the mailbox would cure most melancholies. And if that didn't make you feel better, you could always go into town and buy a whatnot.

Aunt Eunice, Mama's sister, must have been melancholy a lot. I never saw a buttermilk stain on her plaid apron, so I guess she never drank it, and her mailbox was across a busy highway from her porch. A slow walk there was too dangerous—too many pulpwood trucks trying to get to the mill and back to the pines for the next load. Those truck drivers had families to feed and were not on the lookout for melancholy wearing a plaid apron and trying to cross Florida State Road 71.

My diagnosis of Aunt Eunice's melancholy is based solely on her having a houseful of whatnots.

She and Uncle Roy borrowed a house from Aunt Mazie, her sister. It was a month-to-month arrangement that turned out to be lifelong—Uncle Roy's, anyway. They were living there when he died.

Inside the house were racks bought on an easy payment plan in town and wobbly tables bought the same way. Uncle Roy had a folded cigarette pack under one leg of one table to help with its wobbles.

Aunt Eunice had crowded the table tops and racks with tiny ceramic cats and dogs surrounding a picture of an angel helping children across a bridge. There were ceramic birds perched on a blooming peach limb, rabbits with flopped ears, a mouse in a cowboy hat, chickens of every denomination, a calf and his mama, a freckled-faced boy with his fishing pole, and three nativity scenes.

Her collection of ceramics didn't seem to have any theme to their arrangements. For instance, there were birds, cats and dogs all hanging out together. In the real world, seeing a sight like that would be as rare as seeing funeral homes in Heaven. In her mind, Aunt Eunice arranged her colored glass world the way she wished the world really was. And there's no harm in that, now is there?

Mixed in with these unlikely herds was one ashtray to catch Uncle Roy's "Camel" droppings.

At first, he rolled his own cigarettes with the monarchical help of Prince Albert. I used to take his empty tobacco cans and use them as temporary housing for captured grasshoppers. A few times I kept wigglers in them, too. The metal cans were good for that. The lid would snap shut so the wigglers couldn't wiggle out of a fishing trip.

Later on, he switched to what he called "ready rolls." These were already rolled, store-bought cigarettes in foil packs with a picture of a dromedary on the front. He liked Camel brand, non-filtered—he liked to live on the edge.

Only one ashtray was needed in the house because Aunt Eunice made him sit out on the porch to do most of his smoking. As I recall, he did a lot of porch sitting. I didn't know if he enjoyed smoking that much or if he just didn't like whatnots.

I guess Aunt Eunice was aware even before researchers of the negative effects second-hand smoke exposure had, even on a ceramic dog. The smoke stained his spots off-white.

She and Uncle Roy never had children. But they had dozens of nieces and nephews within walking distance to keep her company. And she had Daddy to pray for her "sugar," which is Southernese for diabetes. She also had Dr. Cannon to scold her about drinking too many Coca-Colas.

At least twice a week and sometimes on Sunday they'd summon Daddy to go down there and pray for Aunt Eunice. He would touch her forehead to anoint her with a dab of olive oil he'd bought at the IGA just for that purpose. Probably a little corn oil or melted lard would have worked just as well. The power is not in the oil. It was in the faith and touch.

The Bible says in Exodus 30:22-25 that anointing oils should be pure myrrh, calamus and sweet cinnamon.

Daddy tried to follow the Bible when he could. But myrrh, calamus and sweet cinnamon were scarce in Wewahitchka, Florida, so olive oil would have to do.

He'd anoint her forehead, pray for her, then start retreating toward the porch and the car so he could go home and eat supper.

As Daddy stepped off the porch, Uncle Roy would always ask, "How much we owe you, Woodie?" as he reached for the bib pocket of his overalls as if he had dollars hidden behind a Camel.

"Not a thang in the world," Daddy said. "It's the Lord's work."

Uncle Roy would lean back in his porch chair relieved and fire up another Camel.

All the while Aunt Eunice, wearing her plaid apron, would rock in her chair just out of reach of Uncle Roy's smoke, no doubt thinking about drinking Coca-Colas and buying more whatnots.

Roadside Picnics

BOLOGNA NEVER TASTED SO GOOD

WE NEVER ATE AT the only restaurant in Wewahitchka when I was growing up. I don't know why. We just didn't.

Occasionally Mama would hint how "somebody else's cooking would shore taste good." Daddy never took the hint. So our 4-quart-sized family squeezed in around a genuine artificial woodgrain table inside a pint-sized Jim Walter dining room, passing the dry beans and cornbread, chewing in silence as we ate at home. The only exception was an occasional "Dinner On The Grounds" at the church.

From experience, I knew what those church events held in store. My credentials came from spending my childhood in an Assembly of God church, where tradition dictated that you never passed up a chance to have an "all day to-do." This practice might have become a commandment if Moses hadn't run out of rock to write on.

The scene at the get-togethers never changed much

A few of the men, who smelled like Old Spice and peanut oil, fried fish and hush puppies. The process fogged in the area with savory sniffs that acted as a binding agent of sorts, corralling everyone inside the boundaries of the churchyard, as if they were smitten by the smells and holding hands with a hush puppy.

Two tables over, a woman pulled tin foil off a jagged mountain of fried chicken, in case some finger-licking loafer didn't like fish. She smelled like Crisco and an Avon sample case. Other women were busy popping Tupperware lids off bowls of tater salad and baked beans, all tasty clichés of a Southern "Dinner on the Grounds." The bowls had names taped to the bottom so they could find their way back home.

Standing at one end of the table, I lusted over a 12-layer chocolate cake. Lord, forgive me for my gluttonous thoughts. Then, like a bucket brigade, men started passing dishpans of fried fish and hush puppies, placing them atop strung out sawhorses with sheets of plywood laid on top. These makeshift tables had to be sturdy because asking a Walmart folding table to hold up that much goodness would be like asking a tricycle tire to hold up a loaded log truck. Nearby, just in case someone got clumsy, a dog prayed, waited, and wagged. I know a religious experience when I see one: bream fried crispy so you can munch the tails; old whiskey bottles full of syrup just the right thickness for soppin'; cast-iron pots of peas with boiled okra pods laid out on top like spokes on a chuck wagon wheel; butter beans swimming in bacon drippings, and enough sweet tea to send most every resident at the local nursing home into a diabetic downturn. And don't forget that classic Southern religious experience, nanner puddin'.

Can I get an "amen?"

To say the blessing, the preacher recruited the deacon who never had much to say. On occasions like this, blessings half as long are twice as good. I guess the preacher was in a hurry to climb that mountain of fried chicken. Those church gatherings, eating a kin folk's houses, and an occasional picnic along the roadside just over the Florida/Alabama state line were the only times we ate away from home.

And it wasn't just my family who never ate out.

None of my kin ever talked about eating in a restaurant, either. I guess it was a genetic thing that probably came from both the Martin and Blackman sides. If I had to guess, I'd say it had something to do with money—or lack of it.

I remember Mama complaining about her daddy's "tight purse strings."

And I've seen pictures of Daddy's family during the 1930s. From the looks of them, a dollar bill was as scarce as an indoor outhouse.

My ancestors figured it was just cheaper to eat at the house, and their offspring did the same once they grew up. Besides, if anyone saw you eating in a restaurant, they'd accuse you of just showing off.

Even on trips out of town, we didn't eat in a restaurant. We ate along the roadside.

Several times a year we'd load up on the car (country folks go places "on" the car, not "in" it) for the two-hour drive to visit Mama's people in south Alabama.

Mama would wrap bologna sandwiches in wax paper, put a few boiled eggs in a paper sack and an old cooking oil jug full of sweet tea in another sack, and we'd all get on the Chevy and head north for south Alabama.

My brother and I rode in the backseat.

Daddy always drove and Mama acted as a mobile referee, reaching back from the passenger seat to grab me and my brother during skirmishes. Sometimes she'd extend her reach by packing along what she called a "keen switch." That's a long, flimsy branch—usually from a peach tree—that felt like it had yellow jacket stingers embedded into the bark. Its agility gave it a quick, springy attack, like a rattlesnake strike.

Sometimes Aunt Eunice and Uncle Roy would go with us.

When they came, I'd sit in the back seat between them so Uncle Roy would have a window to blow his Camel smoke out of, and Aunt Eunice would have a window in case she had a "nervous spell."

She could also use the extra floorboard space.

We wouldn't be as far as Kinard before the empty Coca-Cola bottles were clanking around the floorboard under her feet. By the time we got close to Lingo Road outside Dothan, that Chevy sounded like a soft-drink truck bumping down a washboard road.

My brother would be in the front between Mama and Daddy—between a rock and a hard place, the perfect place for him.

As Daddy drove along, he'd look out the window as we passed a pasture and do his bovine-barnyard weather forecast. "When you see cows bunched up like that," he'd say as he pointed toward a passing pasture, "that means a storm is comin'."

"Uh-huh," Uncle Roy would mutter in agreement between puffs.

"Stop looking at them cows and drive," Mama snapped.

Some memories will stay with you for a lifetime and follow you into the dirt. Memories of Uncle Roy will be one of those.

For out-of-town trips with us to visit his folks in Midland City, Alabama, he'd dress in his brand new overalls, his black Sunday shoes but no socks and a shirt buttoned at the collar, but no tie.

He was tall, sun-cured. The skin around his eyes was cracked like the edges of cornbread when it's left in the skillet for too long. He was kind and obliging, and got his and somebody else's dose of patience when dealing with Aunt Eunice's childish ways and obsession with Coca Cola in a bottle.

He smiled a lot, showing his good nature and bad teeth. Years of smoking had turned them the color of yellow dent corn. The neck on my guitar would one day be that same color, and for the same reason.

Uncle Roy sat in the backseat as we bumped along at 60 mph, his calloused, wringing hands in his lap making a nervous, dry paper sound as he rubbed them together.

It was as if he were skittish about riding in an automobile. That fretfulness was justified.

He and Aunt Eunice never owned a car, so he walked more than he rode.

Well, they did own a car for a few hours. But he got rid of it after Aunt Eunice drove it up a camphor tree growing beside Aunt Mazie's house in Wewa. Mama sat next to her, giving her driving lessons. But Aunt Eunice got her gee, haw, whoa, and go confused and they hit the tree and tried to climb it. The car sat there for a long moment, its nose pointed toward a high limb like a dog treeing a coon, before it came rolling backwards.

"You young'uns get out of the way," Uncle Roy yelled. Even at our young ages, my cousins and I already knew how to spot the potential for a good show, so we had gathered to watch.

Uncle Roy never got over the sight of it all, I guess, and never trusted automobiles from that point on. And certainly not while in the back seat of one while Mama was giving out instructions to the driver, even if that driver was Daddy and not Aunt Eunice.

As Daddy drove from Wewa to Marianna and from Marianna to Dothan, there was only one place he was going to stop.

That was a spot a little way past "Possum Trot" store, just past the Florida/Alabama state line, in a shade where the state of Alabama had put up two or three cement picnic tables.

I don't know why he didn't stop at the "Florida Welcome Center." We went right past it! I know they had picnic tables there, too. And free orange juice.

Other than "Donald Duck" brand in a can—which was sour enough to turn you against orange juice and ducks—we didn't have many oranges around the house when I was growing up.

I think oranges must have reminded Daddy of his cold, penniless childhood Christmases in the late 1920s. He often said that all he ever got for Christmas was an orange, and maybe a peppermint stick, if it had been a good crop year. "And we were lucky to get that," he'd say.

Dirt poor memories like that are more than enough to make a feller drive right past a "Welcome Center" orange stand.

But he would stop at the picnic tables under the shade along US 231.

Even before the car stopped rolling, Mama started unfolding wax paper, getting ready to pass out the sandwiches, the eggs and the warm tea as soon as we got out.

There at that eating spot, as Uncle Roy blew smoke rings for entertainment, the scenery was constantly changing from Chevy to Ford, then back to Chevy and now and then, a Dodge.

I never knew boiled eggs and bologna could taste so good, so good that they would have smacked their own lips, if they had any.

It is the best food my memory has ever tasted.

No wonder we never ate in a restaurant!

Burning Needles And Pork Chops

ALL THINGS FAMILY

Mama was the binding agent around our house when my brother and I were growing up.

She was also the head disciplinarian and was fast on the draw when doling out the justice.

I learned that lesson early in life.

If the old Cleckley rental house was still standing, I could take you to the very spot on the porch where she was sitting when I bit her arm. I was about 3 years old.

In a reflex as quick as a snake, she bit me back.

"Now, how does that feel?" she asked, leaving a mark on my arm that looked a little like a toothy parenthesis. My little mind couldn't produce an answer, only tears. And just like that, the "Eleventh Commandment" was written, not on a rock slab, but inside my already rock-hard head. "Thou shall not bite your mama."

Despite what you think about her reaction, she taught me a valuable lesson that day, one I have put into practice all my life: in this life, there are consequences for my actions.

Not only did she bite us back when we needed it, but she also protected us when we needed it. She watched over us the way a mother hen watches over her brood.

Mama even protected us from the dangers we couldn't see by frying pork chops so long that the bone ended up being the tenderest part.

She learned that behavior from watching her mama cook. During the 1930s, that's how they killed the trichinosis parasites in pork—they anointed it with flour and fried it to death.

She protected us in several ways.

Growing up, my brother and I were not permitted to even glance at her butcher knife because Daddy kept it so sharp that just looking at it might cause one of us to slice off a finger.

Mama took care of us by picking splinters from our fingers and feet with a sewing needle. But first she'd kill the germs by holding the tip of the needle over a lit match. It's a wonder she hadn't first anointed it with flour before cooking it to death. The process would smut up the sharp end. But not to worry, she'd wipe off the smut with her fingers before starting any of her exploratory surgery.

After the creosote burned my eyes shut, she made a "tater poultice" to draw out the swelling. She also poured kerosene on my foot when I stepped on a nail, then made sure I got a tetanus shot from Mrs. Gilbert at the health clinic.

Armed with a tablespoon, she force-dosed me with "Syrup of Black Draught" when my stomach ached. Believe me, the ache was the lesser of those two evils.

She protected me on my weekly "Grit Paper" route by not only driving me around to deliver papers but also by helping me collect the 15 cents from a few people who didn't mind cheating a little boy out of last week's edition.

Mama took care of the rest of the family, too.

She washed the "prosperity" smell out of Daddy's clothes using a wringer washing machine and two #3 washtubs. I filled both rinse tubs with water every Thursday morning before leaving for school.

That "prosperity" smelled a lot like the paper mill in St. Joe.

Daddy bought that wringer washing machine on time at Mr. Claude Lister's hardware store in town. The machine reminded me of Dr. Smith's robot on the TV show "Lost In Space." The wringers on those machines had a science-fiction like reputation for trying to eat your arm if you let your mind drift while wringing the water out of a shirt.

That short-legged contraption with a pot belly was the first electric washing machine my folks owned.

For a young south Alabama farm couple searching for anything better, washing machine ownership was a step in the right direction.

I don't know what Mama used back in Alabama on wash day. I guess a bucket of water, lye soap and a scrub board. Then she'd have to wring out the wet clothes by hand. That kind of work made hands strong, which came in handy with it came time to wring a chicken's neck or pinch a little boy who wouldn't be still in church.

Even after moving to Florida and finding the prosperity that came with Daddy's good job, where paychecks were regular and biscuits came in a can, it didn't take a lot of frills to make Mama happy.

Something as simple as a mat'er sandwich made'er happy.

Buttermilk with cornbread crumbled in it also made her happy. As did "The Porter Wagoner Show" and the rasslin' matches every Saturday on Channel 4 out of Dothan.

Babies in her lap and puppies also made her happy, as long as the puppies were in the yard and not in her house.

But what made her happiest of all was her family, her brood.

That included her brothers and sisters, a school bus load of nieces and nephews, and children she babysat over the years so their mamas could work in town.

Just like a mat'er sandwich, her brood made'er happy.

Mama Almost Killed A Lawyer

A TRIP TO THE OFFICE IS NEVER GOOD

I CAN'T REMEMBER WHAT day it was, but I would be right to say it was the hottest day of that summer in 1975. They all seemed that way when you're railroading during the dog days of summer, or at least the creosote made it seem that way.

We were working on the tracks just outside Port St. Joe near the city cemetery, pulling out rotten ties and replacing them with new ones.

I had already heard the rumor passed around amongst the boys about that cemetery. Someone had seen at least one ghost there. That story was used more than once to get girls to ride out there on full moon nights to go ghost watching. The boys hoped the girls would get scared and then want to snuggle if the young men recounted the ghost story with passion and they used plausible adjectives.

We were not ghost watching today. The rest of the railroad crew and I were unloading black, oozing crossties by hand, trying not to snuggle with them, because we knew what that would bring forth. We strung them along the roadbed, one in front of each rotten tie marked with an axe blow from the straw boss.

They soaked crossties in creosote to keep them from rotting as fast.

It had to be Satan's own henchmen who created creosote by cooking coal tar in Hell's own vat. The elixir has the proven reputation of not letting you forget when you get that black fire-without-a-flame on your skin. The exposure left behind little relief and big blisters.

It was enough to cause you to seek a faith healer, as long as the faith healer didn't lay hands on you. Even your forehead was on fire and in no mood to be anointed. Or maybe go back to cutting pulpwood. Anything for some relief.

That creosote smell would not only get on you but also get in your skin, clothes and even in your lungs from breathing the bluish smoke that rose from the ties on scorching days. I can still taste it. It had to be what hot coffee made of battery acid and skunk squeezing might taste like.

"Maybe the rain would wash it off," I thought. It was going to rain that day. I could smell it.

The smell of rain was different in St. Joe than it was farther inland. Here it was a cocktail mix of paper mill smoke and salt marsh that would inbreed and be pushed onshore by a south wind. Everyone knows a south wind is a sure sign that rain is not far away.

But before the rain could get there, a radio call from the dispatcher to my section foreman summoned me to the "big house" in town—the office complex where the railroad honchos gathered to plot against us peons.

I think those bosses saw those of us on the Extra Gang as a grimy, rough-sawn necessity if they wanted to keep their railroad highballing. The Extra Gang handled the railroad upkeep. That job was long on hours and short on pay. The only break we got was during the thirty minutes we got for lunch. And the railroad gods wanted to take that from us. One honcho had suggested that they furnish us with those holders that harmonica players use so they can blow the harp and play the guitar at the same time.

"That way, the harp holder can hold their sandwiches and they can work right on through lunch without stopping," the honcho said.

I guess he was joking. Maybe not.

This was the same boss who told the Road Master to work us five minutes late, four days a week. Then on Friday, let us off on time. "That way they think they get'n off early." That's the same mindset landlords used to keep from repairing a tenant's leaky roof. "When it's raining, I can't fix it," they said. "And when it's not raining, it don't need fix'n."

The dispatcher's voice was scratchy, but the order was clear. "Bring Blackman to the office." To a passerby who might have heard that and didn't know any better, that command could have been a confusing statement, since I was the only white man on the crew that day.

From my experience in high school of being called to the office, I knew whatever was about to happen was not good. This time was no different.

What awaited me was news that Daddy, who I thought of as indestructible, had been knocked from the scaffolding he was standing on at the paper mill. He had fallen 20 feet, landing so hard on the railroad tracks below that one witness said Daddy's belt popped in half on impact. The operator of a boom machine and his flagman hadn't seen Daddy until it was too late.

"They think his back is broken," said Bob Elzie, the railroad superintendent. The news took my breath away as a hundred bad thoughts ran laps through my head.

While it turned out to be serious with a few broken bones, including his hip, his back was not broken. At least that part was welcome news.

Being as stubborn as he was, it wasn't too many months before he was back at work. Doctors said he would spend the rest of his life in sporadic pain from the fall. And he did, especially when the wind was out of the south in August or out of the north in January.

There was talk of a lawsuit. But the thought of going to court scared Mama. She had never been inside a courtroom. It was seldom she even went to the courthouse, except to renew her driver's license, buy a tag or pay land taxes.

She finally conceded, a local lawyer was hired, and they sued.

It would not be legal action against the paper mill, but against the construction company whose machine operator knocked Daddy off the scaffolding.

Daddy would never cast the blame at the wrong feet. It wasn't the mill's fault. Besides, sue the mill that put bread in his family's mouth? The mill who gave them life? To sue the mill would be like suing your birthing hospital because you were born with six fingers on each hand.

If it had not been for that mill, he might still be spending his days in south Alabama, staring at a mule's behind, or coughing lint out of his lungs after working 12-hour shifts at a cotton gin.

"No, sir," he told the lawyer. "Not against the paper mill."

The trial day was set and Mama spent most of her time praying, "Lord, please let something happen so we don't have to go to court."

Day after day, week after week, she repeated that same prayer.

Even as she put on her church dress on court day, pinned up her slip and poked bobby pins in her hair, she prayed that something still might happen to postpone the trial. She prayed on her way to the courthouse. She prayed as she entered the courtroom and was still praying as she took a seat.

Time arrived for the hearings to begin. The bailiff stood and told the judge that they couldn't start. "The plaintiff's attorney is not here," he said.

Mama continued praying.

The judge said he'd give the lawyer fifteen minutes. Ten minutes into the wait, he instructed the bailiff to call that "blankety-blank's" house and find out if he'd left yet.

A few minutes later, the bailiff returned.

"Well," the judge asked. "Where is he?"

"He's on his way to the hospital.," said the bailiff. "He's had a heart attack!"

The judge postponed the trial. God had answered Mama's prayer.

The lawyer recovered, and later the suit settled out of court for a few hundred dollars. I guess a working man's pain was not worth much money back then.

For years, we would kid Mama about the day she almost killed a lawyer. We also joked around about how next time she prayed for "something to happen," she needed to be a little more specific, like the lawyer's car sputtered and stalled—not his heart.

Years later, Daddy retired from the mill. It wasn't these old injuries that brought on the exit. It was more the increasing difficulty he had breathing.

In the beginning, it was Mama who took his breath away. In the end, it was the mill that did it.

He had given over 40 years of his life to that mill, working sick, working holidays, and contracting a lung disease from breathing in that prosperity. The smoke from that good life would take the paint right off the hundred dollar "mill cars" men drove to work instead of their good cars. You could only imagine what it was doing to the workers who breathed it daily for a few dollars. I guess you could call it the price of prosperity.

To show their appreciation when he retired, the mill gave Daddy a pat on the back and a piece of fried mullet.

That was fine with him. The mill had kept up its end of the bargain. It had allowed him to get his young family out of the dirt before they got bogged down between the cotton rows in Alabama. If you're not careful, you can get stuck in a place like that, in a life like that. I've seen it happen. That mill threw Daddy a tow rope so he could pull himself out of that bog and buy things like a Jim Walter house and an almost new Chevrolet. It also put him a notch or two above the bottom, in a place where he didn't have to worry about what a pound of cotton and a quart of sweat might bring at the market that day.

Mill work was sweaty, tiring and dangerous but worth it, because he knew if he did it then maybe his children might avoid a few of life's sharp edges. Most important, the mill had fed his and a lot of other families. So throwing in a piece of fish in addition to all that... well, a working man just couldn't ask for much more.

Not once did he shake his fist at that paper mill, not even when he'd come in most days ground in grime, smelling of dried sweat and "bacon and biscuits"—or at least that is how he described the mill smell. He would come home with his throat blistered from breathing in "something" at work. Unlike some of the other men who contracted lung problems and died before their time, he wore protective masks while painting. But that only postponed the inevitable. He was always grateful for that work because, to him, where he coughed now was still better than where he would have been coughing back in Alabama.

Years later, it wasn't breathing problems that killed him.

With the help of metal cylinders of compressed life and the tenacity he'd gained while plowing mules, he had the emphysema under control—not cured, but manageable.

It was the cancer that finally got him, which I have always felt was just one more legacy of the prosperity he had found.

Drunk With The Chickens

LET US BOW OUR HEADS

DADDY WAS A GOOD man!

One day, a long time ago, I wound up drunk and passed out in my Aunt Mazie Purswell's chicken yard. Why the chicken yard? I guess I was flying high, but not high enough to get back over the fence. I don't know. Ask any drunk person why he slept it off where he did and most times you get the same answer: "'Cause that's where I ran out of stagger."

I must have spent a few hours in there because feathers and other chicken-related paraphernalia decorated me to where I looked like I'd been herding chickens on a barbed wire saddle. By the time my future wife, Susan, dragged me out by the ear, I looked like an old feather pillow that somebody ran over with the lawnmower.

By the time I sobered up, I felt that way, too.

Somebody had boxed my ears until they looked like chickens had been scratching my lobes, looking for grubs. From the taste in my mouth, I must have been scratching for them, too.

Despite that I smelled like the tires on a Budweiser truck after it ran through a chicken yard, and despite that when I opened my mouth to speak it sounded nothing like someone opening a Bible, despite all that, Susan decided I was worth saving.

I guess she saw potential in the drool under the feathers.

I stood up long enough for Susan to lead me from behind the chicken wire. But then I had trouble touching the ground, and felt as if I might fall off the yard, so I squatted and pulled loose from Susan's grip. I didn't want to drag her down with me in case I fell off the edge and landed in a rosebush. So I leaned forward on my hands. Susan backed up to get her shoes out of the way, just in case. I was now on my hands and knees, looking like a dog waiting for a pat on the head after chasing a beer truck and catching it.

Thanks to my nosy Aunt Eunice Anderson who lived next door, and her big mouth, Daddy arrived to witness it all.

When he saw me, he lowered his head.

It could have been bowed as in prayer, but it looked like it was lowered, more like in shame than in prayer. No, come to think of it, it was a bow.

Well, it could have been either, because I was seeing two of everything.

Daddy wouldn't have known anything about it if Aunt Eunice hadn't called him.

"My sister has always been a tattletale," Mama said later.

It had to be disappointing for any man, but especially for a preacher, to look down at this spectacle of a son, trying to crawl out from under a poop pile and sprinkled with feathers just for show.

Mama told me later that when Daddy got home, he walked down the road and cried.

To be honest with you, back then I could not have cared less what Daddy thought.

But that was then. This is now.

Now I could not care more, because Daddy was a good man.

The thought of that day makes me lower my head.

Daddy always tried to do right. His philosophy was simple: if you don't do right, then what's left?

He went through hell, hounds and high water to see that my brother and I wouldn't have to work as hard as he had. Daddy was still working hard so we would have a softer life and not have to swab sweat just to sop syrup.

Daddy knew the wolves were always either on your porch, at your door, or on their way. So he rode every day in a smoke-filled, rusty car to that smoke-filled, rusty paper mill so maybe me and my brother could find an easier way to keep those wolves at bay.

He knew the road to success, the path that led in the opposite direction of stoop labor, was paved with school books.

So he was so happy when I told him I was going to college after high school. Or at least I would as soon as I sobered up from that graduation party where I got my front tooth knocked out.

"Eddie threw a football and knocked it out," I told Daddy as I stood before him with 3-day-old, dehydrated merriment caked in my ears.

But despite that lie, Daddy's heart was still swollen with pride at my collegiate news, so swollen that the buttonholes on his shirt stretched into little smiles.

For my tuition, I'm sure he cashed in some of the US Saving Bonds he and Mama had been squirreling away for their future.

Those bonds were a bantam-size nest egg he and Mama kept in a small wooden chest he built, the lid secured with a dime store lock. They hid the chest inside their bedroom closet under a quilt. They were counting on bad luck not to think about looking under there. But the bad luck was already living in the house with them and would one day dress in chicken feathers.

That fall, I left for college in Tampa.

But my yearning got ahead of my learning, and I was back home before Christmas, still uneducated and now unemployed.

Daddy said nothing about it.

I guess by then he figured it was a waste of savings bonds, time and breath to raise his voice, his eyebrows or his hopes.

He just bowed his head—again.

So I got me a job pulpwooding.

I came home every afternoon in clothes so stiff with pine tar that when I took off my pants, I could lean them in a corner.

It looked like my future was going to be lined with planted pines full of rattlesnakes that struck at anything that moved, like the chainsaw I was running.

Since it looked like that was going to be my high-water mark, nobody bothered to roll up their britches legs.

Daddy bowed his head—again.

It was the early 70s when I told Daddy I was thinking about signing up for my tour of duty on the other side of the world, in a small country divided by North and South, with town names I could not even pronounce.

Daddy bowed his head—again.

But I soon realized that if I was going to have a stranger shoot at me, I wanted it to be for a reason, like maybe after I robbed his store or misjudged his daughter's age. And since nobody seemed to know why the strangers over there were shooting at us, I saw no reason to sign up to be a target.

Later, I started playing guitar in dark places filled with first-hand dreams, second-hand smoke, a lot of music and a little mayhem.

Daddy bowed his head—again.

Then something changed in me. I got saved, not by Jesus, but by a young blond who was willing to step into a chicken yard and lead me to safety. It could also have been because I was older and the older I got, the less I wanted to pull crazy stunts and get got. Whatever the reason, I began to settle down. I went to work for the railroad and soon married my chicken-yard bouncer, Susan.

Six years after we married, I quit the railroad and started playing music full time, still in dark places with a lot of music, a little mayhem and just as many dreams, just not as much smoke because smoke fans had come out by then.

And Daddy bowed his head again, and again, and again.

Through the years, fears, beers and tears, I am thankful that he did.

Daddy was a good man.

First Trip To A Holiness Church

GLORY, GLORY, GLORY!

I WAS RAISED IN an Assembly of God church.

Despite my wife, Susan, saying I'm hard of hearing because of years of playing in a band, I say it's also because I spent a lot of time in that church denomination. That had to be a blame-sharing factor. That and chainsaws.

The Holiness religion is a loud one

At least it was fifty years ago. I think they've turned the volume down a little now.

Susan's first trip to a full-fledged, full-throttled holiness church was as eventful as running over a yellow jacket nest with a lawnmower. And for Susan, it involved just as much motion, just not the pain.

We were in our courtship phase, and I wanted her to hear Daddy preach.

She was used to First Baptist settings which, when compared to Holiness settings, is like comparing the Easter bunny to a Brahman bull.

Daddy was preaching at the Church of God in Wewahitchka that night, filling in for their preacher who was out of town.

The third pew from the front creaked when we sat down.

It didn't take long for the service to heat up.

After about the fifth chorus of "Somebody Touched Me," I could see and hear it coming. I had seen and heard it before.

And Susan was about to see it and hear it for the first time.

I could tell she was getting nervous as people started dancing in place and reaching for the ceiling. They were singing loud and shouting louder. Then a few of them began staggering and falling out on the floor. If you didn't know better, you might have thought someone had swapped the communion grape juice for a bottle of Boone's Farm.

"Isn't anyone going to help that poor man up?" Susan whispered over her shoulder toward me.

"Naw, it's okay," I said. "That happens all the time." The look on Susan's face reminded me of the look on Mama's face when I answered, "Yes, ma'am. I washed my hands."

The lady next to us—who smelled like she might have been the "Church of God" version of the Avon

Lady—began screaming and shaking her head. After being jerked around for a verse, her bobby pins gave up the fight, released their grip and flew through the air like little mosquito hawks.

I think one might have hit Susan.

"While I was singing, somebody touched me..." The multitude sang as the pot boiled.

Bobby pins started flying from other sisters across the aisle. The delirium was spreading like rumors in a barber shop.

Susan nudged closer to me. That part I liked. I was thinking this church thing works better than taking a girl down to the apiary at Cochran's Landing where, on full moon nights, the white bee boxes looked like tombstones. The sight of that, along with a good story, likewise compelled girls to snuggle. Only in church, it was your conscience buzzing in your ears, not the mosquitoes.

What we didn't know was, several pews behind us a child had gotten loose from his mama and was crawling under the pews, making his get-away in our direction.

Pew by pew he tunneled his way, as if guided by a baby Beelzebub on his shoulder, until he was under our pew.

Daddy was skipping around the pulpit like a kid playing hopscotch, wearing out the shoe bottoms he'd just had resoled. He was tossing scriptures around like horseshoes. One scripture, I think it was a Leviticus, hit a sinner and he hit the floor, sprawled out and shaking like someone had poured a bucket of frozen holy water down his shirt collar.

It was getting louder and louder. You could taste and feel the electricity in the air—your tongue tingled and the hair on your arm stood up.

It was like being caught up in a lightning storm, especially for a Baptist girl used to services that sounded more like a drizzle. The closest thing to thunder she'd heard in church was the deacon's stomach growl at high noon.

Susan was wound tight as the girdle the deacon's wife wears to the monthly all-you-can-eat pancake breakfast at Denny's.

And just about the time the service was boiling over the top of the pot, that bubbling little boy, you remember him, brushed up against the back of Susan's leg on his way to freedom.

That's all it took. She jumped up screaming and running in place like she'd stubbed her toe on a mousetrap. She almost levitated off the floor. I saw a roach running for cover.

The lady next to her thought Susan was having a holiness experience.

So, as all Holiness folks do, she plastered her hand on Susan's forehead.

"HALLELUJAH!" the lady shouted. "COME OUT!" she said as if she was casting out that eyeliner devil that had obviously possessed my girlfriend.

My ears rang!

Susan peeled off the sister's hand. The lady put it back. Susan peeled it off again. "No, that little boy grabbed me," she kept saying to Sister So-in-So. But it did no good. The sister knew a future holy roller when she saw one.

Other church ladies joined in. Susan was having to use both her hands to peel the fingers from her forehead.

If I remember right, she was still peeling off hands as I hurried her toward the door.

And the congregation continued to clap, sing and stomp their feet.

"Glory, Glory, Glory, Somebody touched me..... It must'a been the hand of the Lord."

The Lost Highway

GETTING PAID TO PLAY

THERE IS A DIFFERENCE between being drunk on the spirit and being drunk on the spirits. A preacher can help you achieve one, a bartender the other.

Coming from a long line of holiness preachers and honky-tonk singers, I know about both.

Both tendencies are in my blood, which might be why I have this double-barrel craving for fried chicken, the staple food of both callings.

But for whatever reason, when my blood got to the fork in my vein, it went left instead of right. Mama said that left turn was nothing more than a shortcut to hell; the highway Hank Williams Sr. called The Lost Highway—a highway paved with sin, where the centerline is marked in red lipstick and the chicks crossing the road smelled like Chanel; a highway that passed by most every honky tonk parking lot in three states.

Mama and Daddy tried to point me in the right direction. When I was young, I held Mama's hand

and walked with her and Daddy to church three times a week. But when I got older, despite Mama's prayers and her grip, I pulled loose and wandered in the other direction.

Like most mamas, mine did not blame it on the child. She didn't even blame it on the devil.

She blamed it on that drummer in the church band, something Mama hoped I'd never find out. He let it slip that the people down at the Cherokee Tavern would pay me cash to play my guitar there.

To a young man whose future smelled a lot like chainsaw smoke, playing in a bar sounded pretty good. It didn't bother me that it could be more dangerous than a Poulan and could put me in the ditch along the road to Glory. Genetics was already pulling me toward that ditch anyway.

I was already familiar with the Cherokee Tavern through sound, not attendance.

In an earlier chapter, I wrote about how, on Saturday nights when I was a boy, I would lie in bed with the window open and listen. The bump-bump of the bass guitar at the Cherokee traveled through the swamps and ended in my bedroom, as if that was where it was supposed to be.

I was far more familiar with the inside of a church and its parishioners than the inside of a bar and its regulars. At church, people were more apt to hit you over the head with a Bible verse or a fried chicken leg than with a beer bottle or a bar stool.

But inside the church, I wasn't practicing religion. I was practicing my guitar licks. Chorus after chorus after chorus of "I'll Fly Away" gave me plenty of opportunity for that practice.

Feet going to sleep was not a worry, not with a high-test song like that. It didn't matter to the people if your low E string was out of tune, the foot stomping energy kept going and the spirit flowing.

For one old man who always sat in the fourth pew, an occasional trip out to the car kept his spirit flowing. Wearing a red face, a boyish smile and a thin cotton shirt, he would walk by me sitting on the back pew, shuffling his feet and holding his breath so nobody could smell his sin. Everybody knew why he was going out to the parking lot. Everybody knew that the whiskey would one day usher him through the gates of Hell. But everybody also knew one other thing for sure, at least he wouldn't be thirsty when he got there.

He was trying to do God and his wife a favor by staying in the church more than he stayed in the parking lot. But like most mortals, he fell short of that goal. The closer he got to the door, the faster he shuffled. It was like his thirst, his sin, was gaining on him.

My sin was gaining on me, too. But I had nowhere to run. I was still too young to get in the Cherokee door.

I asked for and got paid nothing for playing in church because, after all, it was the Lord's work. But after a while, I figured I'd reached a level where I was worth twice that much. Maybe even three times. That's when, with perfect timing, as if he and the devil were in cahoots, the church drummer let his tongue slip.

It wasn't long before I was smelling like used cigarette smoke and week-old merriment. I had guitar picks in my pocket and guitar licks in my head, with enough money to where, if it cost ten dollars to get to Nashville, I could make it as far as Mama's kitchen table. In my hand I held a Gibson guitar I was buying on time and in my heart I held onto a dream I'm still making payments on 50 years later.

Yes, I was drunk, but not on the spirit or the spirits. I was dizzied by the notion of one day getting paid to play, even if that meant strangers staggering and tripping over my guitar cord.

It was an addiction as powerful as any other. It was even as strong as the one that haunted that red-faced man in a thin cotton shirt; the one holding his breath while he shuffled out to the parking lot.

Mine was an addiction as strong as a preacher's calling and had its own rhyme, rhythm and reason that I'm still hooked on (along with the other half of that double-barrel addiction—fried chicken).

And the preacher said: "As children of God, we are not perfect. Never will be. We've all traveled that Lost Highway and slid in the ditch a few times. You just do the best you can and pray for forgiveness. I'm pretty sure that when God starts deciding who gets through the gate and who doesn't, it'll be like Him reaching into a sack full of skunks, searching for the good ones."

The Word

SHE WAS TOO WISE TO SAY IT

SHE WOULD HAVE TO play second fiddle to his guitar, and she knew it. But that was okay with her.

When they first started dating, she thought the diamond he mentioned might just be the hoped-for wedding ring. But it turned out to be a brand of guitar strings.

But she could hope, despite her parents' warning about falling in love with a musician—especially one who played in church on Sunday morning, straight faced as if God couldn't sniff his breath that smelled a lot like the trash can behind the honky tonk where he had played the night before. I don't think they saw much hope in his future, just chainsaw scars, smoky bars and dry spells between Fridays.

She realized his life might be the theme of prayer meeting sermons and roadside sobriety checks. But that was okay. She didn't have to like the sin to love the sinner. The loving was the easy part.

She knew there would be strings attached when it came to a relationship, and those strings were attached to a Gibson guitar. But she was able to look through the dance hall smoke and see something no one else could see.

That guitar was to be his salvation from chainsaws and spike mauls. But she worried it might one day take him away on a bus with curtains on the windows and its own liquor cabinet—a bus with somebody else's name stenciled on the side, a bus headed toward who knows what or where.

And she knew that one day she might have to choose whether to stay home and be alone or tag along and still be alone because he'd always be on stage or asleep.

Not to worry though. He wasn't going anywhere on a bus. The bus never showed up. Besides, he'd already decided that watching their one-day babies walk across the kitchen floor was far more important than watching some drunk wobble across a dance hall floor, even though both efforts looked a lot alike.

All she had to do was to say "the word" and he would stop playing and take that guitar, hock it and push the picks deep into his pocket. Then walk out the tonk door and dare not glance back for fear that temptation driving an Eagle tour bus might be gaining on him.

But she was smarter than to say "the word." She somehow knew a life without music would suck the life out of his soul. And what good would that do anybody because when a soul dies, everything else around it withers and dies too.

They got married and moved into a house with pane-less windows and cold running water. The planks had been nailed into somewhat of a structure they could stay in as long as he fed the landlord $25 dollars at the first of each month.

Despite the pane-less windows, their life was painless, except for his eyes burning from sweat pouring down from his hatband and his skin set on fire by the flesh-eating creosote fumes boiling up from the crossties.

Then the dream came true! He quit the railroad and became a professional musician, using only his guitar to put bread on the table and car payments in the mail.

But was that her dream, too? The answer to that only she knew!

Then the baby came and the sounds of the restless guitar faded and the Marlboro fog cleared, both being replaced with the dissonance of baby cries and the essence of Desitin.

But they were happy. To him, life tasted like peach ice cream. He still loaded the car with amps, chasing a dream while hauling around a wobbly baby crib that was always missing a screw and had to be re-assembled and set up at the next motel with a lounge.

And off they'd go! From here to there and back. During that time, dreams moved around a lot when they were being chased by a Dodge that smelled like baby powder.

Yet still she never uttered "the word."

She was wise enough to know that music was not an occupation. His past was full of those, from pulpwooding to logging, from counting worms to counting off songs. For some unfathomable reason, she knew that music was more of a calling than a job, almost like preaching. There's not a lot of difference between an offering plate and a tip jar. They are just in different places where people go to forget. And by a God-given gift of foreknowledge, she knew that, unlike last year's Wranglers, music was something he would not grow out of.

So in her wisdom, not once did she say "the word."

But by that time, she didn't have to.

I'd already said it to myself.

She's Married To That Girl

DOING THE LORD'S WORK

LIKE MANY COUNTRY MUSICIANS, I started out playing in a gospel group. That tickled Mama and Daddy. God had answered their prayers—I was not playing in a bar—not at the moment, anyway.

Susan and I had not been married long. On weekends we traveled around to a lot of churches following "The Calvary Trio," the gospel group I played in. We used our own car, bought our own gas, paid for our own cans of Vienna sausages and soda crackers. When you're hungry, those sausages taste a lot better than they smell, as long as you don't read the "Ingredients" label.

The gospel group contained a piano player who sang, two other singers and me, the guitar player who didn't need to sing but sure needed a haircut.

Our venues were small out-of-the-way churches in small out-of-the-way communities where people hugged your neck, whether they knew you or not. These were churches where "dressin' up" for the men meant their top collar-button was fastened and their overalls still had the seats in them. They had callused hands used to carrying chainsaws and choking hoe handles, so when they shook your hand it made your ears ring and you walked away knowing what Elsie's udder felt like after the morning milking.

Congregations were a mix of pulpwooders, farmers, loggers, and wives with okra stings and angel wings, all wrapped up in leathery skin cured by the sun because there are no shady spots in a pea patch.

They were little churches where the preacher had a day job at the local mill where he worked eight hours every day, then visited the "sick and shut-ins" after that. Plus, he found time to tend a garden in self-defense.

The group got paid by way of a "love offering," but in most cases, judging from the quarters and dimes, a better description would have been a "like offering," or worse. Some called it "the love offering tour."

But we weren't in it for the money. We considered it "the Lord's work." In all honesty, though, a little soda cracker money would have helped.

In my 60 year career as a musician, I've been fired twice.

One time it was "The Doc Holliday Band" in Panama City. Doc let me go because I didn't play loud enough.

The second band to fire me was “The Calvary Trio.”

One Saturday my friend, Randy Holmes, was booked to be the special guest singer on the "Cannonball Adkison Show" that aired every Saturday on WJOE, the AM radio station in Port St. Joe.

When Randy sang "Your Cheatin' Heart," he had that same haunting, tortured sound of Hank Williams.. Up to that point Randy was mostly singing to an audience of one—his bedroom mirror. So being asked to sing on the radio was big talk when you're passing the biscuits around the dinner table.

Randy needed a guitar picker for this one gig. I figured if this radio appearance made him a star, maybe he'd drag me along with him, so I raised my hand and volunteered. The following Saturday he sang, and I played at the radio station.

I don't remember just how it happened—maybe somebody got put in jail or broke his hand in a fight—but I wound up being the regular guitar player on that Saturday country music radio show.

The musicians would meet at the station an hour early and cram their amps, guitars, drums and themselves into a room not much bigger than a

McDonald's bathroom. We looked like a bunch of convicts freshly washed, sprayed down and dressed up for church. Once inside the studio we'd tune up and go over a few of the intros so we'd sound like we just flew in from Nashville and our arms were not too tired to play. I was on guitar, Wayne Neel on bass, Marcus Neel on banjo, Angus Peterson on steel, Ronnie Peterson on drums, and any guest stars who could squeeze in. The boss, Clio "Cannonball" Adkison, stood in the middle with his jumbo Gibson guitar, a mic stand and an Elvis-style mic that looked like a chrome trailer hitch with holes drilled in the sides. Like Randy, Cannonball could belt out those haunting Hank Sr. songs as if that "Lost Highway" had stopped right out front in the gravel parking lot. We were the Coup de Ville Cowboys riding on bald tires, looking for the exit ramp that would get us to Nashville.

Every Saturday I was playing there and most Sundays playing in the gospel group.

But then I got caught. The group honcho found out I was playing "the Devil's music" on Saturdays, and the music and band member names were being broadcast all across WJOE's radio land, which only went a few miles in one direction. So the honcho felt compelled to give me the "either/or" ultimatum.

I chose the "or" and got fired for it.

After an encounter with an old woman a few weeks earlier, I think he wanted me to cut my hair too, but never got around to demanding it.

The group was playing at a small church in Kinard, Florida. It was the same church Daddy had pastored when I was a boy.

There wasn't much of a crowd there that night. It looked like Susan and I would be buying our own Viennas again after the show.

I admit my hair was a little long. But not all that long by 1970's standards. And I'd already learned that you can't judge people by their looks. If I'd done that, I would have not had many friends.

But I guess it was long by holiness standards.

"Why don't y'all let the girl playing guitar sang one," said the old woman from the third row. Her voice filled the small church. All the people wanted to laugh. A few did.

Then an awkward silence washed over the room as everyone shifted their eyes toward me, waiting for a comeback.

I tried to smile, but my face looked like a tomato that had been overwatered. I looked at my shoes.

Then I heard a second voice. This one I recognized. It was Susan. She was standing two rows behind the comedian. Her voice was loud and her message was clear.

"I'll have you know I'm married to that girl," she said. Her voice was unabashed and her aim perfect as she zeroed in on the back of the women's beehive hairdo.

When it comes to defending the people she loves, my wife is about as shy as a yellow jacket and as tough as an under-cooked horseshoe.

Laughter filled the little church as the surly, frustrated comedian, dressed up to look like a grumpy old Christian lady, sank back into the pew.

She had been outdone.

We played one more song as the "love" offering plate made its rounds. The group leader cried a sad song, just to add a little drama and maybe compel the people to get out their quiet money, not the jingling kind. It didn't work. They didn't love us very much. In fact, they didn't like us very much either.

When it was over, I packed up my gear, vowed to never cut my hair again, and Susan and I left for home in that Dodge Valiant I had traded an 8-track player and a few Chet Atkins tapes for.

We stopped at a little country store for Viennas and soda crackers and paid for them with our own money.

The Lord's work was over for the night.

Just Married Rental

PULLING STRINGS FOR LIGHT

THE LITTLE HOUSE SUSAN and I rented after we married was only fifty feet from the home where I spent seven years of my childhood. Mama and Daddy borrowed that home month-to-month until we moved three miles south, where their dream of home ownership came true, thanks to Jim Walter financing.

As a child, my cousins lived across the road in a leaky house that Aunt Mazie and Uncle Roscoe also borrowed month-to-month. I remember on rainy days it would have been hard to cook any meals there because it seemed Aunt Mazie had scattered most of her pots across the floors to catch the dripping rain water. I remember each pan had a different tone as the water level rose. It was a symphony of gravity and rain drops sponsored by a neglectful landlord.

On clear days, my cousins and I would roam the roads.

Not far from our houses, land was being cleared for a government housing project. My cousins and I climbed the piles of trees and stumps like they were brushy mountains in need of conquering. On one of those adventures, while I was reaching for a limb, a roach bit my finger. Until then, I didn't know they even had teeth. A few years later, during my heathen years, I would find out that a "roach" could also burn your lips.. But that's a different story.

Daddy built the little house next door to the big house they rented from Mossey Cleckley. I guess Mr. Cleckley was needing more rental property. Daddy probably swapped labor for rent. He owned a hammer and had plenty of sweat, but not much money. Susan and I rented that same little house 25 years later.

It was a sturdy little house because when Daddy built something, it stayed built. I bet he never figured that one day his oldest son with a new wife would call it home, for a little while anyway.

This is the same house where Susan's sister cried when she first looked through the front door. "My little sister is going to be living in here?" she said between sniffles.

The yard was full of camphor trees, just like the yard next door where I ran around with a towel cape, pretending I could fly. White oak snakes love camphor trees. They also seemed to love coming inside your house.

More than once Daddy had to drag one from behind the commode. Looking back now, I'd say that would have worked better than Black Draught for curing constipation.

That was along the same time the bathtub fell through the floor and hit the ground—Daddy, water, washcloth and all. I'm just glad our dog wasn't sleeping under the house that day. Just like at Aunt Mazie's house, gravity and water were something to contend with. Only in this case, Daddy's pan had four claw feet and rust stains.

Not long after Susan and I moved into the house Daddy built, I heard her screaming from inside the bathroom. "THERE'S A @&*#* SNAKE IN HERE!" I'm sure if her sister had been there, she would have cried again. Since white oak snakes are non-venomous, I just shooed him out the back door.

The next day, while she was in the backyard hanging out clothes, I heard Susan scream again. That same snake, or it might have been its twin, curled up atop the clothesline post, eye-level with her. I had to kill it because it just wouldn't leave Susan alone. Not that I was concerned for her safety. I was more concerned with mine if I didn't take decisive action with a hoe. Plus, I just got tired of hearing her scream. I'm pretty sure the neighbors did, too.

It was a small house. The living room was almost big enough for two people, a couch and a TV, including its metal ears covered in tinfoil.

The security system on the front door was a propeller latch made from a piece of wood nailed to the door facing.

Sometimes, when we went out and shut the door behind us, the latch would bump around and lock us out.

No problem.

All I had to do was lean on the door and the nail that held the latch would pull loose and the entire security system would hit the floor.

The kitchen was small but big enough to hold the stove we bought from Daddy's sister-in-law, Aunt Lois, and the refrigerator we bought out of the front yard of an appliance repairman we found in White City. We had no trouble finding his house. Old appliances covered his yard like Maytag mushrooms.

There were shelves in the kitchen, but no cabinets. Being raised in a Jim Walter house, I already knew that the size of the kitchen didn't matter because frying bacon smelled and tasted the same no matter where it got its start.

At least the bathroom was in the house.

At first we had no hot water. Before the next rent day came, Mr. Cleckley had a water heater installed. The rent shot up to $25 a month. That was fine because cold showers took the heat out of the newlywed romance. Snakes in the house will do the same.

The bedroom had no closet and was missing a couple of panes in its only window. The room did have a clothes chest that Susan pushed in front of the bedroom door for security when I left before daylight to go railroading. That extra security made her feel better because you never know when an intruder might lean on the front door.

Even though we had to pull a cord hanging from the ceiling to light our path, the house that Daddy built was feeling like home.

Considering everything, we were lucky.

I had a job, and Susan was going to hair-cutting school, driving to Panama City every day in an old Dodge Valiant.

With its slant-6 engine, the Dodge ran as quiet as mouse snores.

Not counting its looks, the only other downsides were that the steering had more play in it than an Aussie puppy, and the roof lining sagged and threatened to squish Susan's hairdo. So she had to drive to Panama with her head tilted as if she were trying to drain water out of one ear.

I made enough money at the railroad to keep us in the "Just Get'n By" column. But any extra dollars were as scarce as turnip trees.

And, like most newlyweds, sometimes we had trouble making the dollars beat the month to the finish line. But what's new about that?

As they say, "Trouble will always find your door, visiting the rich and the poor. To face up to it, you are duty bound to not offer it a place to sit!"

Since our couch was so small, there was no place for "trouble" to sit down, so it never overstayed its welcome.

For weekend entertainment, we sat on the floor at our bedroom window with the lights out on Saturday night. From the "good seats," we watched our neighbors who lived in the same house where me and my folks had lived.

Yep, some might say, "Spying on your neighbors, huh?"

But like I said, it was for entertainment, not nosiness.

Almost every Saturday night, the large husband would stagger home around midnight. The smaller wife would lie in wait behind the door and waylay him with a frying pan, then get him in a head hold as he wobbled across the threshold. We had to shush ourselves to keep from picking sides and cheering them on. All we needed was popcorn.

The scuffle never lasted for more than a round or two before Police Chief "Preacher" Glass would arrive, snatch the frying pan from her hand and give her husband an "or else" talk, and the show would end.

It wasn't us who called him. Honest! We were being entertained, so why would we call the law? That would be like unplugging the band's amplifiers right in the middle of watching a hawk and a chicken slow dancing.

It was a visual adventure.

If I had to explain now what it looked like then, what comes to mind is a big Clydesdale and a little bitty yellow jacket being in the same horse trailer at the same time. In situations like that, size don't really matter.

I guess you had to be there to appreciate the spectacle.

As you can see, other than each other, Susan and I didn't have much. But to us, the world looked just fine, even though we were viewing it, not from the bottom up, but pretty close to it.

It didn't matter to us that we had to pull a string to turn on a light or that our security system needed a bigger nail.

We were young. We were busy hammering out a life, hoping that the nails would hold, just like they did in the little house that Daddy built.

But living in that house, I came to realize one important thing.

Men build houses. Women build homes.

Traveling Troubadours

BEST PICKER IN THAT DARK DEN

He just couldn't seem to find my eyes, so he spoke to my nose while we stood in the Gold Nugget Lounge in Panama City.

"B-B-Bill... you g-gonna be able to d-d-drive home?" my uncle said, his hand on my shoulder to steady his world.

He'd played music somewhere that night. He was weaving so much that it made me dizzy just watching him. I had not one drop of liquor that night. But after watching him weave like he was steering an old Ford tractor, if I had closed my eyes, I could not have found my nose with the tip of my finger. Not even if the off-duty deputy sitting at the end of the bar had ordered me to.

On this night it was plain that when my uncle left home to go play music, he walked steadier going than he did coming.

As far as I know, he never had been shot at and hit. But both he and his Corvette had been in jail once—locked up by a North Florida sheriff because of missed child support payments. Daddy arranged bond and got him out.

Despite the wobbles, he was still the best damn guitar picker in that dark den of nuggets that night, including myself.

With six strings, wires and wood, and with his eyes closed and his teeth grinning, he could do more than most of us pickers could do with our eyes open and gritting our teeth. His talent was a magical elixir made from a jigger of guitar and two fingers of Chet Atkins.

Race-horse fast on that guitar neck? No. But he was a tasteful player, knowing when to pick and when to be quiet. The tone from his guitar was like peach ice cream—cool and smooth and made you want more.

He was past the age where white hair should have taken over his head. He had weathered a few storms that came in half-pint bottles and others that came with lips as red as that tempting apple preachers mention when they're reading from Genesis.

No, his hair was not white. It was black and shiny, like an undertaker's shoes. Curled a little in the front were a few strands dangling over his forehead, like Elvis' did. The sides were wavy and swept back over his ears like he'd driven a Harley to Happy Hour.

A drummer once told me he just couldn't understand it. "I can tell a lady a joke to get her attention, and all she'll do is grin, drink the gin that I bought'er and walk away. But your uncle wouldn't have to say nothing. He'd look up from his guitar neck like a shy little boy caught looking at the bra pages of a Sears catalog, grin a little, and look back down at his shoes. That's all he had to do to attract ladies like nails to a magnet."

He never smoked, not on his own anyway. Like the shots of tequila between songs, the crowd furnished it all without the inconvenience of having to buy his own Marlboros or settle up a bar tab at the end of the night.

A lot of guitar players I know, including myself, would drive people to stagger and dance in honky tonks on Saturday night. Then on Sunday go down the road a bit and drive people to shout and stagger in church. It was our apology to God because we knew there were only a few breaths and a severe case of scented hiccups that separated hell from hallelujah and "last call" from "altar call."

If he ever played in church, I don't recall. He might have, because after all, it was in his blood. Maybe

I was lazy that Sunday and missed it. Or maybe I was there but dozing on the back pew. I hope not. I would hate to have been there and missed him twanging through the smokeless air for a change.

But it didn't matter if he was sitting on a church pew or a barstool. He could make that guitar talk and do it in a language that people understood.

He and his carload of troubadours full of ballads and bullshit could draw people out of their seats. The dance hall would be full of swaying paper mill workers and housewives, pulpwooders and school teachers, nail drivers and hairdressers.

That night at the Gold Nugget even my former Sunday School teacher was there, backsliding across the dance floor with her once holiness hairdo now relaxing on her shoulders. I didn't recognize her—almost. Any preacher will tell you that there are only a few dance steps separating honky tonk heaven from holiness hell. And those corn-meal-sprinkled dance floors made it easy to slip from one to the other.

"Damn," I thought as I stood on the stage and watched her. "I wonder if she's gonna be teaching Sunday School tomorrow morning?"

The place was packed that night. They were all there for the same reason.

Just so a few pickers with buzzing amps and a singer on a scratchy microphone who sounded a little like Merle could help them dance away the working man or woman blues. And do it until midnight was a memory and it was almost time to go teach a Sunday School class.

No Need To Pay To Pray

MIRACLES ON THE PAYMENT PLAN

EVERY HOUR HE WAS awake, Daddy was a plow mule for Jesus. He probably plowed with his eyes closed, too.

So many times, and at all hours, he would get a phone call from Aunt Eunice to go pray for her—the sound of a radio preacher blaring out his mailing address in the background through the phone static.

Not once did I hear him grumble as he slipped his work boots back on, grabbed his dog-eared Bible, the anointing oil from a high shelf on the bookcase, and go out the door. The oil came from the IGA in a bottle labeled "Olive Oil."

Sometimes, if it wasn't too late or too early, I'd get to go along.

It's funny when you think about how miracles can show up in unexpected places—for instance, along State Road 71 outside Wewahitchka, Florida, in an old house and a porch with wooden steps that sagged when Daddy stepped on them. He'd always grab a post before putting his full weight on a plank, just in case his faith in wood stumbled and failed.

Uncle Roy would be there, sitting in a rocking chair bought on time from Danley Furniture Store in Port St Joe, a non-filtered Camel dangling from his lip as he slipped off his work boots. He also smoked while putting them on that morning.

He worked on the state road crew and was outside all day, so he could smoke while he flagged traffic or danced with a weed sling, and do it without making anybody cough.

With his boots sitting empty next to his rocker, his smoke was swallowing the porch as we arrived. I couldn't help but sniff it as we walked past him, either that or hold my breath. What I didn't realize then was that walking through the smoke was advanced training for my one day playing in smoky tonks.

"Y'all come on in," he'd say through the smoke with one eye squint. "She's in the house."

I will never know what a real camel stinks like. But I remember what his Camel haze smelled like—leaves burning.

Inside, the house had more of a lip-smacking aroma. I guess because of all the fatback she had fried in the kitchen, the smell had soaked into the planks, even the ones in the living room. Of course, it helped that Uncle Roy seldom smoked in the house, only on the porch.

I called it a miracle on SR 71 because Aunt Eunice said she felt better after a "laying on of hands" by her ordained brother-in-law.

So you can say what you want, believe what you will, but that put Daddy having more success as a healer than the doctor or the radio preacher. And both of them wanted her on a payment plan before they'd even attempt a miracle.

Mother's Day

I MADE IT HOME OKAY

Hey Mama,

I know it has been a year since I last wrote to you. I think it was on Mother's Day. So you see, I'm no better at writing letters now than I was back when Susan and I were on the road playing music.

I just wanted to check on Daddy since the doctor gave him the long face about his cancer. Is he preaching anywhere this Sunday? Is he still excited about going to Heaven so he can find his mama?

I realize we just talked on the phone a few days ago. But I know how much you like to get letters. So here you go, I wrote you one.

You and I wrote back and forth a lot when Susan and I were on the road chasing that musical dream like a dog chasing a pulpwood truck, not knowing what we'd do to keep it from running over us if we did catch it.

Sometimes it took a little while for those letters to chase us down. We moved around a lot then had to forward and sometimes backward our mail to wherever our next gig was.

At least that's the excuse I used about why I didn't write you back often enough. You were right to complain. Of course, you were right about most things.

Not that I didn't appreciate your dispatches from home. They were as refreshing as a double-scoop ice cream cone on a summer day. Butter pecan is my favorite.

What made those letters so good was that they always included a progress report on Daddy's garden, or how full Sister Scott's fig tree was this year, or how Brother Bailey brought y'all a hamper of peas that didn't have too many snaps this time.

There's nothing better than getting a letter from home. Especially when you're living in a glorified closet with a double bed. Those rooms were a carbon-copy of the last glorified closet we were in somewhere on the other side of North Carolina. I swanny, each room looked exactly like the last one, right down to the same color bedspreads and curtains, an open suitcase on the bed and a seldom-used Bible in the top drawer. Everything looked and sounded so much alike that sometimes when I woke up in the morning, I didn't know if I was here, there, nowhere, or somewhere else. I just knew it wasn't somewhere special.

Your letters from home were like warm biscuits on a January morning. It didn't matter if they were wearing syrup or not. In my mind they still tasted like home and filled the empty spot in my heart and soothed the homesickness gnawing in my gut.

How does Daddy's garden look this year? I remember one year him looking out over his bumper crop of pigweed, nutgrass and thistle, and saying, "I think that last gooanner I bought must'a had weed seed in it." Who knows, he might have been right. I guess "gooanner" was his Alabama pronunciation for guano-mix fertilizer.

Oh yeah, before I forget, Happy Mother's Day!

Susan and I always have had a hard time deciding what to get you for Mother's Day. This year was no different. We hope you will use the new knives and not store them away for a dull day. Ha! Ha!

One year we gave you a new set of spatulas. That Christmas, you gave them back to us, unopened. You had wrapped them in what looked like reused wrinkled paper with crinkled drawings of baby Jesus on it. The Christmas card had some unknown person's name at the bottom almost covered in white-out. You had scribbled "From Kat and Woodrow" over it. Frugality? I guess old depression era habits are hard to break.

Looking back, I figure there's one thing we could give you that you might use—ringside tickets at the

Dothan Farm Center to watch the wrestling matches.

Maybe advanced tickets to the "July Fourth Battle Royal" where promoter Rock McGuire always assembles a good lineup of your favorite heroes and villains: Dick Dunn, Bad Boy and Billy Boy Hines, The Masked Infernos, and Mario Galento and his brother Spider.

Maybe even a special guest appearance by Andre the Giant, ducking his head to get through the door and stepping over the top ring rope while the regular-sized wrestlers were having to go under it.

Just think, from your folding chair sinking in the sawdust, you could shake your finger only inches from the nose of that cheating Mario. You'll be so close that he can smell the Jergens lotion on your hands. That would be much better than poking your finger on the TV screen from your Jim Walter living room, sitting in that Naugahyde-covered ringside seat a hundred miles from his actual nose.

The only other time I remember you touching the TV screen was when you were helping Oral Roberts pray for a drunk who stumbled into a revival tent outside of Tulsa.

Yep, I believe you would like the live wrestling match. One good thing about it, it would be hard for you to re-gift it next Christmas.

Ole lazy me, I started to send you the same "Mother's Day Letter" I wrote to you last year. Maybe it wasn't laziness that caused me to even consider it, but just that re-gifting gene you passed on to me. Ha! Ha!

Well, it's finally daylight, and I've got to go feed the horses, so I'll close.

Maybe it won't take me so long to write you next time. I know you would like that.

But before I disappear into the barn shadows, I want to thank you and Daddy.

"For what?" you probably think.

For y'all's prayers. Without them, and that set of Western Auto jumper cables Daddy gave me, I don't know where I'd be on this Sunday morning—probably stuck on the side the road somewhere between halos and honky tonks.

I know y'all pray for me all the time, even when I was playing in church and not those cloudy honky tonks. Some people believe in prayer only when the weather is stormy. You and Daddy believed in prayer on the clear days, too.

Tell Daddy I'll be praying for God to heal him. Tell him he doesn't need to be in any hurry to go see his mama. She's not going anywhere.

Still your slow-to-write-you-back, loving son,
Billy

PS: I made it home alright from playing last night in what you call "one of them places." You always want me to let you know when I make it home okay.

Sane an Sober

BARSTOOLS AND PEWS

DADDY NEVER ONCE ASKED me to stop playing in bars. I know he wanted to, but he didn't. In his quiet thoughts, I'm sure he wished I'd taken a different path, one without so many briars.

A young preacher in Panama City did once tell me I needed to stop playing in honky tonks because of all the "bad things" that went on in there.

My first thought was not whether he was right. I knew he was kinda right. I also knew he was kinda wrong.

"Have you ever been inside one?" I asked.

"No, sir," he said. "I have never and don't plan to ever darken the door of one."

"Then how do you know what all goes on inside one?"

In one sense, he was right, but "bad" might be too strong a word.

Inside those doors the thick smoke and dim light from the blinking beer sign behind the bar makes every woman look like an angel, gives her wings and makes her cowboy hat look like a halo, or at least it does after midnight. And I've seen it enough times to know that whiskey can buck cowboys off barstools and send them flying to the floor where somebody steps on their hands.

At the end of the dance floor, on a stage held together with duct tape and nicotine glue, is a band called "The Cadillac Crusaders." They have whiskey on their breath and whiskey in their voices. As a group, they are as country as homemade hominy as they dazzle the crowd with a homemade harmony they bring with them to the gig bottled in half pints.

The band could make it in Nashville—they are almost that good. They are not bright stars yet. More like flashlights shining through a smoky dream, but they could find work. There wasn't any band in Music City any better than them, only luckier.

One night an almost sober promoter tried to get them to load up in his car so he could take them straight to The Opry. Their chance had come. It was staring them in the face with car keys in his hand. But they just couldn't do it.

"I have to be at work tomorrow," the guitar player said. "I have a baby to feed."

"Yea," said the drummer. "I got twins."

To them, their babies were more important than their dreams. They loved their babies more than themselves. I told you they were good.

So they settled for a dark corner in a dark place once a week.

There they sing of tear-stained pillows, tortured souls, and lost loves. Every hour they take a fifteen minute break that lasts thirty. Fifteen minutes is just not enough time when the bass player is trying to convince a certain lady that he would be a safe bet if she were looking for more in her life than a one-night barn dance. The last time she heard a sales pitch like that, she ended up buying a used car with sawdust in the transmission.

The guitar player and drummer play at the holiness church every Sunday morning because Baptist music just doesn't have much of a beat. Playing in a bar one night and in church the next day keeps the devil confused as to where to find them—at least that's what they hope.

These tonks are as American as AppleShine. Everyone in there stands when the band plays that Lee Greenwood song. And everybody, I mean everybody, claps after a Merle medley, because Haggard was the hero who sang about them and the struggles when you mix memories, misery and a quart bottle of gin that somehow holds a gallon of demons.

Yes, the whiskey sometimes brings on insanity of varying degrees, or draws it to the surface, anyway. It was already close to the surface when they got there. It was just hiding in their sweaty shirt pockets behind a pack of Camels, or in the women's purses under the breath mints.

Nobody knows what brings out the silliness, whether it's the beat of the bass drum, which you feel more than you hear, or if it's the whiskey, which you also feel more than you hear as it's sneaking up on you.

Maybe it's just the melodic mixture of the two that builds until it reaches critical mass and boils over like a stopped-up toilet just before it hits the fan.

Or maybe it's a lifetime of stoop labor with no promise of anything better that makes people crave a taste of insanity. It helps them forget.

Sore backs just make the night more volatile because the only relief comes by soaking your muscles in alcohol, from the inside out.

Inside those tonks, an anti-American sentiment is as scarce as a full set of teeth and as dangerous as a chainsaw with a full tank of gas and an empty conscience.

This is a place where the harder you drink, the softer you step, whether you're on the dance floor or sneaking back into your house after closing time, trying not to wake the wife.

Yep, the young preacher was right to think that "bad things" do sometimes go on in there.

But he was also wrong.

Inside that cinder block building is also a gathering place for good, hardworking people with sweat lines on their caps. Their hands are calloused from pulling wrenches—their knuckles banged up and dyed black from the motor oil ground into their skin. They are as no-frill as a bottle of wine bought at the grocery store, and they will gladly gang up to help push your car out of the ditch at the end of the night. The challenge is getting them to all lean and push in the same direction at the same time. They change their own flats and eat out of their own gardens and sometimes go to church with whiskey on their breath and throbbing memories they'd just as soon forget.

They are as generous as they are poor. On the bar, in front of that blinking beer sign, sits a jar full of dollars and dimes, collected to help the family living not far from the bar after hard times caught up with them, ran over them, then backed up and ran over them again, just to be mean.

Nope. Angels ain't always sane and they ain't always sober. But they are still angels. Some just happen to sit on bar stools instead of church pews. And I'm sure when the angelettes get to Heaven, they'll want to sit in with the Heavenly Choir and sing that Tammy song, "Stand By Your Man."

Maybe Daddy knew that, too, and that's why he never said anything to me about playing in what Mama called "them places."

Daddy's Last Sermon

THAT OLD WELL

LAST NIGHT WAS A good night to sit outside and listen to the darkness.

It was quiet. Mother Nature seemed almost speechless. It was a good night to have a conversation with God since it was so still you could have heard a sin drop.

All I could hear was an occasional old memory rattling around inside my head. I thought I also heard that sparrow in the laundry room. She builds a nest in there every year. But I know for sure that I heard my neighbor's dog barking in the distance.

When something gets the dogs' attention, most of the time the neighbor's dog is the second barker in a chain reaction where our dog, Honey, is the first to sound the alarm. But this time she slept right through it, whatever "it" was.

This quiet time would be a good time to scribble down a few writing ideas. I have a pencil and paper with me, just in case. Sometimes I have trouble unscrambling my scribbled thoughts because they look a lot like sparrow tracks on the dusty sill in the laundry room window.

I could be more productive by making paper airplanes and, from my porch rocker, launching them off the porch, trying to ring what's left of the old well now being used as a burn pit. It's kind of like a game of horseshoes except closeness doesn't count. This forces me to have to climb out of my rocking chair roost, stumble off the porch and pick up the paper because my airplanes never land where they are supposed to.

Daddy always talked about that old open well. I think it conjured up unbruised memories of his childhood before life had a chance to put a headlock on whatever youthful dreams he might have had.

I know life started out pretty hard for him. It was that way for most people during that long dry spell called "The Great Depression."

But he got through it and lived a good life when you consider where he started and where he ended. His life started out smelling like sweaty mules and cotton poison and ended up smelling like roses and honeysuckle growing in the ditches along the "Streets Of Gold."

It was the autumn of 2001 when Daddy got the long face from the doctor, followed by the words "pancreatic cancer." The COPD he'd traded paper mill paychecks for had already landed him in the hospital several times.

His doctor said his lungs were full of holes, "like swiss cheese," he said. That corrosive mill smoke had eaten holes in them the same way it ate holes in the hoods of those old mill cars. But, with his breathing treatments, Daddy had the COPD somewhat under control. He had to give up his harmonica playing. But he could still spit fire from the pulpit and singe the hair around the Devil's ears.

The doctors just couldn't figure out what was causing the pain in his side. Maybe it was from that old injury when a boom machine knocked Daddy off a scuffle at the paper mill, they thought.

But that wasn't it.

The source of the pain was coming from behind his liver, hiding like the coward known as cancer will sometimes do. I never heard Daddy say how long the doctors gave him to live. To him, it didn't matter—death did not frighten him, not one iota. God had furnished him with a pair of wading boots so he wouldn't get his feet wet, and he was ready to cross Jordan.

"The first thang I'm'a'gonna do when I get to Heaven is to go find my mama," he said several times. He almost seemed excited about it. Like a kid on his way to Disney. "How much farther? Are we there yet?"

Daddy was in his bed on October 15, 2003, when he heard his final trumpet, a sound that only he could hear. He was 83.

He was lying in his own bed, inside his own bedroom, inside his paid-for Jim Walter house. That's where he would have wanted to be. I guess God answered one more prayer for him.

Mama told me that two nights before that, while she and my brother were in the living room visiting, she heard Daddy preaching from his bed. It was about 9 o'clock, she said.

"He preached on and on solid until around 4 in the mornin'," she said. "He mentioned thangs I ain't thought about in years."

Then, with his earthly vessel now drained and his last sermon preached, he collapsed into his bed, closed his eyes and never opened them again.

I wish I'd been there to hear his last sermon. Lord knows, during my childhood I sat through enough of them I didn't want to hear. Then, on this one night when he was preaching one last time, I was in Tallahassee and missed the one I wanted to hear. The one I should have heard.

The next morning, I drove to Wewa. He was already knocking on death's door by the time I arrived at his bedside. He just hadn't stopped breathing yet.

I shaved him because I knew he would want to look his best when he got to stand face-to-face before his Savior. Besides, what would his mama think if he showed up needing a shave?

His breaths grew weaker and farther apart as Mama leaned over and used her fingers to comb strands of his hair. Her tears were raining on his face, painting it in grief that glimmered in the sunlight that washed through the window. Her tears ran down his cheeks, wetting the pillow. It almost looked like he was crying. But he was too far gone for that. Besides, what was there for him to cry about—it was almost suppertime and he was almost home. (If he had been, it would have been the first time I ever saw him cry, even though I knew he had that time he saw me drunk and lying in my Aunt Mazie's yard. Mama told me so.)

For over 60 years, Mama and Daddy took care of each other. Some of those years were tough. But even those poor years produced a rich story that only they could tell.

They were married on November 30,1940, eleven years before they moved to that farmhouse on the edge of that cotton field near Enterprise, Alabama, in 1951—the year I was born.

Since that time, he had never left her alone for any extended period. For all my life, they had just always been there.

Now, for a few more breaths on this earth, they were still together.

"Don't leave me," Mama cried.

It broke my heart to see her this way.

As my brother and I stood at his bed, Daddy's breaths got farther and farther apart. Then he quietly stopped breathing. He was gone. After decades of making a stand against the Devil and all forms of sin, warning nonbelievers of a fate hotter than an August cotton field, God called his faithful servant home. It was time for our daddy to go find his mama.

Still crying, Mama stood up and walked to the end of the bed. There, I watched her do the most loving, endearing thing I had ever seen.

She felt of Daddy's cold feet sticking out from under the quilt, reached over to the dresser at the foot of the bed, pulled out a drawer and brought out a pair of socks. She then slipped them on his feet.

Who else but a loving wife would put socks on her dead husband's cold feet?

Eleven years later, on a bitter January day in 2014, Mama died following a fall in the nursing home. She was at Bay Medical Center in Panama City for several days after the fall while doctors tried to save her from a brain bleed. Because of the blood thinners she was on, they couldn't stop the bleeding. They gave up hope and put her in a room in the hospital's "Hospice" section. They expected her to live only a few hours longer.

But she refused to give up. Days and days passed.

It was on January 22nd when Susan called with the news that Mama had died. I had come home to rest and Susan was sitting up with her at the hospital. I was expecting the call, but still wasn't ready for it. We never are.

Why did she hold on for so long after doctors said she should have passed days ago? Why January 22? Susan and I were baffled.

"Oh, that's why," we said almost in unison after we remembered that January 22 was Daddy's birthday. She was waiting until his birthday to cross Jordan and be with him again. This time not in a farm shanty on the edge of an Alabama cotton field, or in a rental house where snakes congregated in the bathroom, or in a Jim Walter home on the easy payment plan. Now, throughout eternity, they would hang their halos on Heaven's hat rack every night and not have to worry about cooking supper, mill whistles or packing lunch buckets.

What a wonderful birthday gift Mama gave Daddy that year!

To me, that gift was even more a show of love than putting socks on his cold feet eleven years earlier.

What You Remember, What You Don't

DISHPAN UTOPIA

FUNNY WHAT YOU REMEMBER and what you don't.

I remember the last time I saw Daddy sitting up in his living room.

He was in his favorite chair, high on his pain meds because the cancer had robbed him of everything but the pain.

Growing up, I never saw him sit down much, except to put on either his work shoes or his Sunday shoes. Since he was a preacher, I guess you could consider his Sunday shoes his work shoes, too.

On Saturday afternoons, he would sit long enough with Mama to watch "rasselin." Now that was entertainment. Not watching the TV, but watching them watch the TV. They'd both holler, scream and cheer for the "good guys" and Daddy would threaten to take a 2x4, jump in the car and drive the 100 miles to the Farm Center in Dothan and "straight'n' out ole Billy Boy Hines," one of the bad guys. Their tangy, reverberating commentary could be heard all the way to the intersection of Pine Avenue and Second Street. Lord, what did the neighbors think?

When I look at pictures of Daddy during his younger years, I wonder what he dreamed of, what he hoped to become. I'm sure he didn't want to spend the rest of his life being dragged around in the dirt by a brain-dead, one-crop mule.

In old pictures I can see by his hat that he liked a "Gus crease." Genetics are funny, I like a "Gus crease" hat too. I have two of them.

There's one old picture of him standing out front of his neighbor's house. With dirt on his clothes and no doubt dust up his nose, he looked as if he'd just stepped out from behind a mule. He had what appeared to be a "Gus" hat in his hand. As he looked into the camera and held his breath, he was no doubt daydreaming, not about a better future where every Sunday smelled like fried chicken, but about more important things, like maybe getting to drink his water in the shade for a change.

On this last day I saw him, Daddy was sitting in the shade inside his Jim Walter home in Wewahitchka.

He was upset and pointing to the ceiling on the other side of the room.

Over the years, during rainstorms when the wind was just right, the water would get under the old, blistered shingles and leak. That water would drip on the tiles and leave dark circles, kind of like the dark circles left on the ground where you park a Ford with a leaky transmission. He daubed the white ceiling tiles with even whiter paint, trying to hide water stains. But the white paint made the flaws even more noticeable because it drew your attention to them. Kind of like putting white lipstick on a not-so-white hog.

Later he had the roof recovered, which stopped the leaking. But the old daubed-over evidence remained and remains to this day, looking down on whoever sits in that room.

That day, thanks to his pain-free euphoria, Daddy thought it was raining again and the roof was leaking again.

Mama kept telling him that it was not raining and the roof was not leaking.

"There ain't a cloud in the sky, Woodrow," Mama said. "The roof ain't leaking."

"Yes, it is! You see! It's dripping on the floor," he said as he leaned forward in his chair and pointed toward the dry carpet.

Mama, being Mama, kept arguing with him. "No, it ain't!"

Daddy kept on fretting and pointing.

I walked into the kitchen and grabbed one of Mama's dish pans, the big one with the dents in the side. It was one of those all-purpose pans you can wash dishes in, like the name implies, or shell peas or even wash a baby in. I took it into the living room where Mama and Daddy were still arguing like newlyweds and put it on the floor underneath that leaking roof to catch Daddy's medicated hallucination dripping from the ceiling.

All was quiet again. Daddy leaned back in his chair and dozed off, his mind relieved because at least now the floor won't rot.

Then I said those words I now regret. "Well, I guess I'd better get on back to Tallahassee."

"You don't have to go yet," Mama said, just like she'd said the last hundred times before I left. "You don't have any chickens to feed." That was my granddaddy Martin's excuse he used when he was ready to end his visit and go back to south Alabama. "I gotta feed the chickens," he'd say, walking out the door.

I had something just as important to do.

Or at least I thought I did.

What I realize now is that what was important was dozing in his chair, now relaxed because I had put down that real dish pan to catch his mythical water.

Funny! I can't even remember now what was so damn important that I had to get back to.

What I do remember is that the next time I saw Daddy, he was in his bed, his eyes closed, only minutes away from dying. I felt like going to the kitchen and grabbing a dishpan to catch my regrets before they rotted the floor.

That Mill Check

PULLING A GRADE

THE PAPER MILL TOOK Daddy's harmonica away.

I put it back in his top shirt pocket as he lay in his casket so it would be handy when God gave him his new lungs.

Well, the mill didn't really take the harmonica from him. But it took away the breath he needed to play it, and if you ask me, that's the same thing.

But he never balled up his fist and shook it at that paper mill for taking his breath away. Instead, he folded his hands in a grateful gesture for what it had given him.

The mill had fed his family. That job had given him the ability to hold his head up in front of anybody, proud because his family had never gone hungry. To him and his kind, "Thou shalt always take care of family" was a commandment Moses forgot to chisel into the rock.

That steady mill check enabled him to buy at least one new '56 Chevy and two like-new Dodges, but never a Ford. I'm not sure why. Could be it was a lingering depression era grudge for Henry Ford because he replaced men with machines. Maybe?

That mill also allowed him to buy a house that he mostly had to rebuild. On those back door steps is where he'd sit with a bag of oysters, shucking, smacking and celebrating his good fortune.

Though life wasn't a bowl of peach ice cream, it was close to it.

He had a harmonica in his pocket, oyster stew simmering on the stove, and we had a hambone in our dry beans.

But by no stretch were we rich. To think that would require stretching your imagination so tight that the Devil could use it to bounce back up and onto Heaven's porch. Rich folks in our lineage were as rare as watermelon trees.

But Daddy knew, or knew of, a few rich folks. He had worked for at least two.

One was Mr. Ed Ball, who owned the Apalachicola Northern Railroad and the paper mill in Port St. Joe.

The other one was the owner of the Alabama land Daddy plowed and tended in exchange for a portion of the harvest. The landowner also owned the old clapboard house where Daddy and Mama were living when I was born in 1951, it leaning at the edge of a Coffee County cotton field. But it was rich dirt. It just had a poor man plowing it.

Word that the paper mill in Port St. Joe was hiring drifted north, just like the smoke from its stacks. The smell of good fortune lured him south with a promise of more to hold on to than reins hooked to the steering end of a mule he didn't even own. The mill offered him things you might find in a workingman's picnic basket. There was health insurance, paid vacation, a retirement plan, and a steady paycheck that didn't depend on the finickiness of an unpredictable beast and weather with the same disposition.

So he laced up his old work boots, the ones with the past stuck to the bottoms, and moved his young family south toward the future. He settled his new family in Wewahitchka, renting a house well within driving distance of his smoky salvation that he couldn't see from there, but could smell when the wind was right.

It would have been nice if he'd had a better pair of boots for the occasion. But you really don't need new boots to take a giant step forward. So he just wore what he had.

I'm sure he'd already caught wind of how the paper mill smoke was so corrosive that it would eat the paint off the cars sitting in the parking lot. I doubt it would have mattered if he'd known in advance that it would do the same to a man's lungs, but at a much slower pace. That was just the cost that came with the paycheck, not only as peeling paint on the hood of a mill car but also a cough that just wouldn't go away.

If that's the price he would have to pay, then so be it. He would pay on it a cough at a time—a little at a time, the same way he paid on Mama's new wringer washing machine.

Before the emphysema, he had the wind to call up a steam locomotive with that Hohner harmonica. He'd inhale to get the lonesome sound of a far-off train whistle, then inhale and exhale real fast to get the sound of the engine pulling a grade.

Then it seems he just got up one day and was inhaling and exhaling, puffing not into his harmonica, but into a plastic hose over his nose.

Beside his chair was a small electric motor plugged into the wall, puttering and straining as if it were out of breath, clicking along like any other Medicare breathing machine.

Over the next few years, his harmonica migrated from his shirt pocket—where it was always handy in case he needed to whip it out and pull a grade—to his dresser drawer where it lay out of sight, out of memory and out of breath.

That's where I found it on the day of his funeral.

And I slipped it into my shirt pocket so I could slip it into his as he lay in that casket. You know, just in case he might need to pull a grade—just in case Heaven was on a hill.

Paper Walls

COLD BISCUITS AND HOT COTTON ROWS

THE MEMORIES ARE EVERYWHERE inside Mama and Daddy's old house.

They are in the walls, the floors, the ceiling, and in old shoe boxes sitting on top of the cedar chifforobe. Memories are even in that kitchen drawer where Daddy kept screwdrivers, a claw hammer, pliers, a Crescent wrench and loose nails and screws of all sizes. The screwdriver with the wider end served double duty as Daddy's oyster knife. Yes, he had a good job so he could bring home a bag of oysters at least once a year.

The memories are everywhere and they are as comfortable to me as my old barn shoes.

On the table next to the bed, where Mama left it, is a copy of my first book. It was read once and was once red, but now is faded pink from the morning sun that leaks through the blinds.

That ordinary table came from Danley Furniture in Port St. Joe. To me, it is now extraordinary, if for no other reason than for the round stain on top that I put there when I was a child. I don't remember what was in the glass I set there, I just remember how much trouble I got into for doing it. Even cheap tables are expensive when you're on a paper mill budget, so they needed to be respected

Owning even a non-fancy house like this one was an answered prayer for so many people back when Mama and Daddy arrived in North Florida from south Alabama.

If they could pull it off, home ownership would be a way of getting back at an early life when their future looked like it might be filled with cold biscuits and hot cotton rows.

Despite the odds, they were going to have a home that belonged to them, a home without a landlord knocking on the door on the first of each month. Well, it would belong to them one day, as long as they kept up with a payment schedule that came around in monthly circles, just like a landlord.

They had worked their way through and outlasted the hard times. It's kind of like how grass will work its way through an asphalt road no matter how many times it's run over. Those were hard times my brother and I never had to wrestle with. We came later, and by that time I could not have cared less about listening to the sweaty history of it all.

Because of that, the memories I have of the house taste like ice cream. I didn't care about the rocky road my parents had to endure to get us to that point. That trip was their vision, not mine.

Now, when we stay there, I sleep in the same room, in the same bed and on the same side of the bed where we watched as Daddy's breaths faded away. In that bed is where he left this earth as quiet as a sparrow flying out through a laundry room window.

When I wake up there now, I sit up on the side of the bed where Mama had laid her forehead and begged Daddy not to leave her. Her tears puddled on the floor in the same spot where, the other night, I spilled water I was sipping. The memory was sharp, and I avoided stepping on it out of respect as I went to get a towel.

Mama and Daddy were together for over 60 years. Most of those years were in that Jim Walter house. When you're in a place for that long, memories can't help but soak into the floors.

The first time I saw that little house was when I went there with Daddy so he could give their dream the once over before signing the papers. I must have been around seven years old.

The house had a walk-on porch not much bigger than the cooter hull of the Chevy we came in.

In his mind, I know Daddy was already building a big, screened-in porch. After all, when you are building a dream, you always start with the porch and work your way back.

The previous owner had covered the inside walls with flattened cardboard boxes. He nailed them in place as if they were expensive wall covering from Sears instead of rejects from the box plant in Port St. Joe where he worked. But they got the job done despite the words, "THIS END UP" printed on the boxes with the arrow pointing down.

The kitchen/dining room combo was so small that an average-size man could stretch out his arms and come close to touching two walls at once. Sometimes when I'm there now, I can still smell the gravy Mama made from coffee and bacon grease. And if my reverie was hungry, I could still taste it, too.

There was not even enough room in there for a refrigerator. It sat in the living room like that visiting uncle who always had room for more groceries.

Over the years, they added two more rooms, expanded the kitchen and moved the refrigerator into the kitchen where refrigerators feel more at home.

That gave us more room in that little living room that needed all the room it could get.

In that living room on Sunday mornings when I was a teenager, Daddy sat in his chair and I sat across from him on the couch. Our knees almost touched as he watched Brother J.W. Hunt preach on the TV. I held my breath so maybe, just maybe, he wouldn't smell the lingering bouquet of Miller High Life—that is, as long as I didn't belch.

Daddy would sit there during the commercials and turn his attention toward me, preaching about the downfalls of staying out past 11 the night before.

I used to hate those sermons because they forced me to hold my breath until my face turned red. What I wouldn't give to hear him preach to me again.

That Old Bible

AN ANTIDOTE FOR THE WORRY LINES

WHILE IN WEWA THE other day, I spent time in the middle bedroom at the old house, sitting in a straight chair, thumbing through Mama's Bible.

Her Bible shows signs of wear over many years of use. Inside it has more dog-ears than our backyard the time that girl dog showed up with her entourage.

Lord only knows how many trips to church and back that Bible made. But I guess mileage is a quality you like to see in Bibles and barn shoes—something with the new wore off; something that molds itself to you and you to it; something that just feels right to your soul and soles.

Flipping through the pages, I found underlined scriptures that no doubt meant something special to her.

I have a feeling I might have been the reason she underlined some of them. Maybe those lines were a reflection of the worry lines I put on her face.

She underlined a few passages in red ink, others in blue. I guess she used whichever pen she had handy that day. No doubt many of the passages she marked were from the hundreds of sermons she sat through as Daddy preached long and loud, but never boring. During those services, she'd sometimes stand because I figured she was close to "get'n happy." Or maybe it was just those hard pews. After a while, everybody welcomes an opportunity to stand and give his or her backside a chance to regain and reclaim its piety, perspective, and circulation.

Inside that middle bedroom, the straight chair was as hard as the church pew. Like those pews, it creaked when I stood for a moment to regain and reclaim.

The room was so quiet. All I could hear was a memory, echoing and faint, as if coming from a tomb deep inside the frayed Bible.

Squeezed between the pages and chapters of time were things not only important to her, but turns out, important to me, too.

Somewhere in Genesis, I found a Valentine card from Daddy. His fading signature was barely readable, written by a righteous left-handed man who could barely write. His words were hard to follow. Daddy's penmanship looked like sparrow tracks scurrying across the ground because a cat was nearby. Next chapter over, I found a copy of his obit, along with his "25 Year" certificate from Tupelo Masonic Lodge #289.

A few pages later, I found some of my old newspaper columns. The paper was brown and brittle and only a sneeze away from being scattered across the floor into a thousand memories to be swept away by either time, a breeze or a broom.

Two chapters later, I found a collection of answered prayers mashed between Joshua and Judges. If you think about it, what better place to store proof of a few answered prayers than inside an old Bible?

There were birth and graduation announcements of children, grandchildren and great-grandchildren. I found a warranty card for a car battery installed in 1972, and a payment card for a "Maytag" wringer washing machine, the words "PAID IN FULL" stamped above payment #24 like the brand of an honest man. There were birthdays and death days scribbled on the backs of old electric bills. And I swear, on one page, the tantalizing smell of fried chicken propelled me back in time. But it could have been just my stomach's memory deciding to get involved.

Before now, I was never sure which one I believed in the most, prayer or blind luck. After looking through this Bible, I have now moved my straight chair into the amen corner. I've often joked that if not for my parents' prayers and a set of jumper cables, I don't know where I'd be today. There might be more truth in that than I first thought.

Bad luck has a way of tumbling with the grace of a cinder block and causing an avalanche of other cinder blocks to join in. But prayer can do the same thing. You run out of luck after a while, both bad and good. But one thing I can say about Mama, she never ran out of prayer. She was fast to anoint my head with a prayer when needed. She was just as fast to anoint my hind end with a switch when needed.

It's hard to tell which one had the most influence on me.

Probably the prayer, because she firmly believed God answered them. I guess I do too. How else would I explain why I'm still above ground after a lifetime of smoky bars and loud guitars, "tequila shooters" and at least one potential shooter with a gun in his hand? He came into a bar where I was playing and pistol-whipped a guy. Why? I figured it was personal, and I didn't ask for any details as he ran back out the door after delivering his message.

Prayer is a potent force. How else could you explain why I'm still walking upright after more than once-in-a-while driving home late at night and not even remembering how I got into the car? Throw in the years of flesh-eating chainsaws, Murphy's Law, and mares that kick first and ask questions later, and you walk away with believable scars and a belief that prayer works. And in my case, it worked overtime.

Things like that are not marked on specific pages or in scriptures underlined in ink inside her old Bible. But they are still a powerful testament that prayer works.

Hindsight helped me see that while I was sitting in a quiet room inside their Jim Walter home, I can see that now.

Especially now, since I am grown, she is gone, and I still have the foresight to seek the things she saved inside her old Bible.

Trip To The FRM

PREACHNG TO THE CHOIR

IF DADDY WERE STILL alive, I wonder what he and I would talk about if we took my old truck into town to the feed store. We used to do that most every time he and Mama came to visit.

I wonder what he'd have to say.

He wouldn't talk party politics. As a survivor who tasted the cotton dust and felt the sting of "The Great Depression," he was a lifelong Democrat. Period.

Southern men of that dirt poor time blamed the Depression on Republicans.

They even named that bumpy, poke-salad period in history after a Republican, calling them "Hoover Days" in dishonor of President Herbert Hoover, who showed up at the wrong time.

These hard times created a new lexicon among poor folks.

Newspapers that covered people sleeping in the streets became known as "Hoover blankets." Small communities of starving families were called "Hoovervilles," and residents renamed armadillos "Hoover hogs." I guess attaching the word "hog" to an armadillo improved the taste. Or made you think it did, anyway.

When it came to endless cotton rows, holey overalls and hoe-handle blisters, they pointed a gnarled finger like the calloused barrel of a scatter gun at all Republicans.

There was nothing political to talk about, so he didn't.

Sometimes, while sitting on a porch, he and his friends would discuss local politics. But they limited it to remarks like, "Well, old so-in-so started going back to church, so he must be gonna run for re-election." Either that or the law or an ex-wife was looking for him.

I don't remember Daddy once talking about national politics. To him, they all smelled like skunks wearing Old Spice to mask their true nature, and talking about it left him wanting to spit. Kinda like when you take a big swig of soured milk without first testing it with your nose.

On our trip into town, he and I would stop by the corner store. There he'd buy me and him a Dr Pepper. I'd buy us each a bag of pork rinds—barbeque for me, plain for him—just like we had always done.

When we'd get to the feed store, we'd both pause on the porch for a second or two, not saying anything, just sniffing the air. There is nothing that'll get your soul right faster than the smell of sweet feed, brooder biddies, and fertilizer dust, all mixed into one inspiring inhale with your mouth closed. You didn't dare sneeze for fear of losing the moment.

As I would pick out the feed, he would stand gawking at the seed bins. He'd peep inside each one as if being seduced by names like "Yellow Dent" and "Silver Queen." As far as I know, this was as close as he ever got to a corny, porny peep show.

On the way home, he'd talk about Jesus and how we are living in "the last days" before the rapture. Daddy took his Bible straight up with no chaser. He'd come down hard when it came time to choose sides. If you weren't part of the choir, so to speak, and didn't like what he had to say, you'd better move your feet fast or get your toes danced on.

We'd ride a little farther, then he'd tell me how St Joe hasn't looked right since they tore down the paper mill smoke stacks—didn't smell right, either. Then, after a pause, he'd continue about how commodity cheese tasted best and how he couldn't believe my old truck was still running.

I'd talk about playing music, my garden and how I learned the hard way how important it was to plant by the moon signs, just like he'd told me. I'd tell him about the head kick I got from that old dun mare, and how the late frost stunted our pear crop this year. And together we'd wonder why we hadn't heard many whippoorwills lately. If he'd thought of it, he would have blamed that on the Republicans, too.

When we'd get back home, we'd sit on the porch and he'd tell me again the dangers of that old open well being so close to our front doorsteps.

"It's hard to move a hole and even harder to move a house," I'd say. "And when I take a shovel and fill it up, the dirt disappears after it rains."

"Get'a bigger shovel."

We laughed, and I'd change the subject by pointing out how these porch boards he and I nailed on years ago were holding up pretty good.

And before long noon would catch up with us, and he'd rock and begin sermonizing about Susan's cornbread. The smell of it frying had sneaked its way out of the kitchen and was leaking out through the screen door and into his thoughts.

"I could make a meal out of just that," he'd say about the cornbread. He always had something good to say about Susan's heavenly Hoover Mill creation. I guess he figured the owner of that mill was a Democrat.

And I'd have to remind him that, on the subject of Susan's cornbread, he was preaching to the choir.

The Letter

FOLLOWING THE SPARROW TRACKS

DEAR DADDY,

Yesterday I found what looked like a sparrow feather in the pasture.

While walking along, spreading out piles of hay for the horses, I looked down and there it was. I almost stepped on it. There were a few tracks around it, so I was pretty sure it was a sparrow's feather. I know what sparrow tracks look like because I see them on the windowsill in our laundry room. A mama sparrow builds a nest in that cat-less domain every spring. She gets in and out through the open window. Her tracks on the sill are pointing toward her nest or pointing away from it. It takes a lot of trips to keep those mouthy young'uns of hers fed.

I figured finding that feather had to mean something special, so I looked it up on the Internet.

"Angels communicate with us in a range of different ways, such as feathers appearing in our path," said the article. "Finding a sparrow feather is a good omen. It means you are being protected and kept safe in many small ways by the spirit of a loved one who has passed. And if you're lucky enough to see tracks, take note of the direction of travel and follow that path in your daily life because it is your angel who is guiding you."

Was it you who put that feather there? Or was it just some bird that's going bald? Please don't tell me that.

It was you, wasn't it?

I believe God sends angels to this earth to help guide us through the storms. And those angels don't always have wings and wear halos. Sometimes they crave cornbread and are covered in fleas.

You never got to meet our dog, Honey. You had already gone to Heaven when I found her half-starved.

Well, to be honest with you, it was more like nine-tenths starved.

I wouldn't have found her if unexpected rain hadn't run me home early that day. Was it you who sent the rain? She was lying in the middle of the road. I thought she was a rag and was about to straddle it with my truck. The rag saw I wasn't going to stop, so it got up and staggered to the ditch and fell down again. As if she thought being in a ditch might save her from my sometimes erratic driving.

The steering in that truck has more play in it than a box of puppies.

"That rag is a dog!" If I had to describe what she looked like, I'd say she'd been to hell and back twice, and just did made it out this last time. She had to be only hours, maybe minutes, away from becoming a buzzard's buffet.

Hair and bones and not much more. Her skin crawled with a thousand fleas. Her eyes were half shut and weak. She was close to giving up. Death has a stale, rotting smell to it, and she smelled like it. Kind of like the waiting room in a funeral home, or the garbage can out back. As my friend Frank Morrison would say, she looked like death sucking on a Life Saver, whatever that looks like. Where did this cocker spaniel come from? At least that's what I thought she was. It was hard to tell under all those fleas. She wasn't lost as much as just misplaced by some happenstance that I can't explain. The same type of drizzling happenstance that ran me home early that day.

Besides, to be lost, you've got to first know where you're supposed to be. From the confused look in her weak eyes, she didn't know where she was or where she was supposed to be. But wherever she was supposed to be, it wasn't in a ditch along a dead end road. I left her there and drove the half-mile home to get a can of dog food, my pistol and a shovel. I figured if she'd eat the dog food, she had a chance. If she was too far gone to eat, well... I'd take the pistol and do what I didn't want to do and call it kindness. After eating all the dog food, she licked the empty can. I put her in the back of the truck and brought her home. She cowered in one corner of the truck bed, not knowing if her good luck had finally run out, or if her bad luck was just hitching a ride to the end of the road.

We washed her. Well, Susan washed, and I held on in case she thought we were trying to drown her. The rinse water was pink, as if every flea had to spit out a mouthful of blood so it could hold its breath to keep from drowning during the soapy storm. Her very life was dripping from the ends of her ears and soaking into the ground.

We drowned a lot of fleas that day.

That afternoon I took her to the vet at one of those walk-in, no-appointment-needed dog clinics.

From the stares, you would have thought I'd walked in carrying the welcome mat that had been stomped on too many times, the one laying out front of death's door. The vet on call looked at her, looked at me, then looked at the floor and shook her head. She walked off without saying much, other than "She's pretty skinny." "I hope she's not going to charge me for that diagnosis," I whispered to Honey.

The vet walked back in with a needle to draw blood. She said nothing. She didn't have to. I could read the words in her eyes.

"Mister, you're wasting your money on this one. She probably won't see tomorrow. Definitely not the day after." If the vet had written out a prescription, it would have said, "Take one shovel and dig one hole..." The blood the vet drew wasn't red. It was a pale pink like watered-down lemonade. Blood tests showed she was anemic and full of heartworms, stomach worms, and other worms I'd never heard of. It was a "who's who" list of infestations that had hitched a ride into town that day. The vet didn't give her much hope! In fact, she gave her no hope at all. She doubted this matted package of bad luck would make it back to the house. But what the vet didn't know was that at our house, we don't give up on things when somebody throws them away because they have a little wear and tear on them. I put Honey back in the truck cab, which more or less confirmed she was now family.

Back home, I tied her on the porch—didn't want her wandering after wondering what I was going to do next. She was weak and had severe diarrhea. We fed her people food, including Susan's cornbread. Over the next few days the diarrhea slowed to a trickle, then stopped. The cornbread had worked its miracle.

I've always said Susan's cornbread could cure most any ailment, even a bullet wound if applied internally and soon enough. Daddy, I remember you felt the same way about it.

Honey was too weak for conventional heart worm treatments that might kill her in the process of killing the worms. We had to come up with a workaround.

A horse client told me that small doses of ground black walnut hulls would kill the heart worms without killing her. She had nothing to lose. She couldn't get much lower unless I dug the hole first. So I started the treatment.

A few months later she tested heartworm negative. I guess heartworms don't like black walnuts.

She drank water out of the pool and wanted in the house when it was thundering. She would let me know when a summer storm was coming long before I ever heard it. I guess she worried what would happen to her if something happened to me.

To watch her, you'd think she'd been assigned the job of being my protector. She'd try to bite anybody who came into her yard carrying a pamphlet or a clipboard. Armadillos and foxes sometimes kept her awake at night and her barking kept us awake, so we'd bring her inside. We named her Honey because she was the same color at Tupelo honey. Then we threw her more cornbread because Honey and cornbread are a tasty team. Is that what angels eat for breakfast?

Honey was a full-blooded cocker spaniel. She had to have belonged to somebody. We had the vet scan for a chip. No chip. We uploaded her picture to the local "Lost Dog" sites. No response. So she became ours. Or was it we became hers? I guess it depends on if you believe in angels. Later, we expanded her name to "Honey Bunny." I guess that expansion was natural when one sees life as one gigantic poem, sometimes rhyming, sometimes not. This time, it rhymed. And what about some reason to go along with that rhyme? Well, you can forget about that if you're trying to come up with a reason a stray rain shower sent me home early that day. Daddy, I think you know the answer to that. (wink-wink!) Besides, sometimes it pays to not spend too much time trying to figure stuff out. Instead, just go about your daily routine and realize that sometimes angels end up right where they are supposed to be. Ours did by living a half-mile down the dead-end road from that ditch where she found me.

Despite what the vet predicted, Honey lived 10 more good years. That's a lifetime for a dog..

Over those years, she brought us a lot of joy and protected me from lightning and pamphlets.

If she wasn't an angel, she missed a good chance.

We could use a lot more angels on this earth right now.

I don't know if you've been keeping track of what's going on in this world, but we all could use more watching over and guidance.

There have always been dark spirits among us. But not like we are experiencing today. I think somebody forgot to close Hell's gate.

If you were here now, you wouldn't recognize the world. I'm even having trouble recognizing it. It all leaves a gnarly taste in my mouth.

I can't count how many times you preached about the last days before the Lord starts his roundup. The way I figure it, He's tightening the cinch on His saddle right now.

Maybe looking down from the high seats, you have a better view of what's happening. But looking up from my porch vantage, it makes no sense to me. But I fear it makes sense to somebody who's eating breakfast with Beelzebub every morning while planning his day.

I already know what you would say about all this turmoil in the news.

"Told y'all so," you'd say. "I told y'all we was livin' in the last days!"

Over the years, I heard you preach about that so many times. I wasn't always asleep on that back pew like you thought. Besides, it's possible to have your eyes closed and your ears open at the same time.

It was hard to doze through your preaching, anyway. Some preachers were as dry as a sawdust sandwich and as quiet as a gnat's wings during take-off. Not you. You'd stand up behind that pulpit and preach and dance in place, then scoot across the floor and preach some more.

"Soon God is going to slam His hand down on the arm of His chair and say 'Enough is enough!' Blow that trumpet, Gabriel, and let's go round 'em up."

Then, with perfect timing for dramatic effect, you'd slam your hand down hard on the top of the pulpit just as you said "... slam His hand down...". It sounded like a shotgun went off inside that plywood box. I'd jerk my head up from examining my shoes and look up real fast to see if a squirrel or the Devil might fall from the light fixture.

It sure looks like you might end up being right.

But you did your part by sounding the Biblical warning and, in the same sermon, showing that not all hope is lost.

I hope you know you had a positive influence on many people who still remember you. One of them is me.

Instead of pouring a bucket of shame over my head that day I was drunk in Aunt Mazie's chicken yard, Mama said you walked down the road and cried and prayed. I am sorry now that I put you through that then.

There are many other times I disappointed you.

You gave up your today so that my brother and I might have a tomorrow full of sunshine, shade trees, and peach ice cream. You'd come home every day smelling like the paper mill, sit in the same chair, take off your work boots and set them in the corner. It was like all the smelly backaches of that day were trapped inside those boots, and you could set them off to the side and forget about it until 4 the next morning. It's too bad it took my nose so long to catch wind of all you sacrificed.

So, I'm glad I found the sparrow feather to remind me. I'm glad you put it there.

And I'm glad the sparrow left its tracks. I noted their direction.

Your eldest son,

Billy

Whispering
GHOSTS GATHER AND WATCH

He walked around the room with the baby in his arms, while ghosts with the smell of snuff on their breaths watched over his shoulder to make sure he was doing it right. He carried the baby close to his heart. And he whispered.

The old ways that used to be handed down through time are vanishing, like a foggy morning once the sun comes out.

It used to be that old superstitions were as much an heirloom as old cookbooks and family Bibles—keepsakes to be passed down over and over to the next and next generations.

"Don't bring that hoe into this house, it'll bring bad luck with it!" I remember Mama saying that as my young brother, who for some unknown reason, was walking through the front door with a hoe in his hand. My brother and I have kidded each other about that for years. "Steve, don't you bring no hoe into this house. You take her somewhere else." Mama never caught on. At least, we hoped she didn't.

"Birds singing at night bring bad luck" is another one. I guess it never dawned on anyone that many songsters do a better job after the sun goes down, or at least they think they do. I've seen this same phenomenon many times on a honky-tonk stage.

If your nose itched, company was coming. If your right eye itched, you were going to be glad. If your left eye itched, you were going to be mad.

Though these beliefs are steeped in tradition, deep down we don't believe them. But then again, who wants to take any unnecessary risks with so much at stake? So we kinda believe because our parents did, as their parents did, and so on up the line.

Sometimes I repeat them when the right situation comes along, or I'm just feeling nostalgic.

I read of an interesting superstition the other day, one that Mama and Daddy didn't practice, at least not that I remember. But who knows, I was pretty young when I was born, so I wouldn't have remembered it anyway.

It used to be when a new baby was born and brought home, chosen family members, like an aunt, uncle, grandparent or trusted friend, would gather at the home and take turns carrying the baby.

They would amble and circle the room, holding the newborn near their hearts and whisper things to the baby.

You weren't supposed to tell anyone what you whispered because doing that would break the magic. Kinda like telling folks your wish after you puff out the birthday candles, or wishing out loud after you see a star fall out of the sky.

As each person totes the baby around the circle and whispers, the good qualities of that person are said to be absorbed into the baby, like the warm sun on a chilly day.

Even though somewhere in the past it was probably a part of my people's beliefs, I had never heard of this practice.

But who knows, my kin might have toted me and my brother around the room.

Some traditions we might still do except that we just forgot how, like buck dancing, skinning a squirrel or checking the moon phase before we plant potatoes.

Four years ago, when my grandson was born, I restarted this tradition. I didn't tell his parents what I was doing because they have a college education and you know how education can drain the taste out of a superstition.

I walked around the room and whispered to my new grandson. I'm sure the ghosts of my people were looking over my shoulder, just to make sure I didn't sour this ancient and important tradition.

These would be the ghosts of hard men humbled by the bundle they once carried. Hard men with a soft touch when holding their babies. These men were as tough as a hickory hoe handle and as stubborn as a mule stuck in reverse. Their knuckles were swollen from a lifetime of labor, so swollen they could hardly fit their hands into their pockets to reach that Case folding knife they always carried—just in case. These were not-so-holy men dressed in holey overalls that smelled like sweat and Sloan's liniment, the cloth worn thin like the seats on their old pulpwood trucks.

And alongside them would be the ghosts of mamas, grandmas and great-grandmas. They draped themselves in homemade dresses that looked a lot like feed sacks with buttons sewn on just to make them presentable. These dresses had at least one side pocket big enough to hold two cans of snuff and a King James New Testament.

All these ghosts would gather around for one purpose: to watch and make sure I did this thing right.

I've Googled every keyword I can think of and can find no information on this practice, or just which people brought the tradition with them when they starved across the ocean.

Is it true? Can a baby absorb good qualities?

"Don't be silly!" the pessimists will say.

I don't know! It might be true! But what I believe is that when we touch a baby, whether it's to kiss a cheek, palming a forehead to check for a fever, or carrying a baby around a room, that touch is a point in time where the past touches the future.

There are just some things both believers and pessimists will never understand. But who wants to miss a chance to have some of your good qualities be absorbed by a child?

Besides, it's hard to suffer from pessimism when you are holding the antidote in your arms, close to your heart, touching his ear with your lips and whispering.

Sparrow Tracks

FINDING DADDY ON THE FLOOR

I ALWAYS FIGURED THAT if I shook his old Bible hard enough, Daddy would fall out!

One day I did, and he did—sorta.

There wasn't a lot that fell out when I shook it.

But everything that did reminded me of him—two page markers with Bible verses printed on them. A loose page from Deuteronomy floated to the floor along with gas receipts from Boddye's Standard Oil station across from Border's liquor store (A man could get himself and his car gassed up without having to walk too far). In the pile was also a receipt for preacher dues paid to the Assembly of God District Council in Marianna. Daddy never charged to preach, but the District Council charged him to preach. He was a good Democrat. He paid his dues to the District Council and to the United Paperworkers International.

On the floor was a birthday card signed "Woody" he'd given Mama and an old pay stub from the paper mill in Port St. Joe with something scribbled on the back. I couldn't make out what it said—the lines had faded. But it looked like it might have been a pencil-drawn map to a cinder block building of lost souls somewhere in south Alabama. I couldn't make out what he'd written on it. His fading scribbles looked a lot like sparrow tracks across a dirt road, weaving this way and that, but always moving in one general direction.

To me, that pay stub represented a Greyhound ticket receipt wrapped in a metaphor. It even smelled like the paper mill. That paycheck gave Daddy and his young family a ride from the cotton rows of south Alabama and dropped us off at a better place. While that better place wasn't quite Heaven, it was a lot closer to it than the over-plowed place we'd come from. A little rental house under the camphor trees in North Florida allowed Mama and Daddy to taste what the people in the big houses were having for supper.

But I didn't need to shake that Bible to find him. I just needed to look inside.

When I opened it, there he was, in the spaces between the columns of printed words in the Book of Matthew. I'm as close to being a Bible scholar as a water hose is to being a water moccasin, but I think it was the spot that talks about how God knows and sees everything, no matter how small, even a sparrow when it falls.

In those spaces between those columns were little scribblings in dark ink. It was notes written by Daddy, no doubt for a sermon planned for whatever Sunday that page landed on.

I couldn't make out all that he'd written. But that was okay, He could. And God could too.

Daddy could write, but barely. His ink marks across those pages looked a lot like those same sparrow tracks on the back of that pay stub.

But I guess for a poor farm boy from Alabama during a time when fieldwork was more important than school work, he wrote well enough to get by.

The people of the dirt who stooped every day and smelled like mule sweat and cotton dust needed a little education, if for no other reason than self-defense. There have always been people who would cheat a man who couldn't read, write, and do a little math. But armed with just a hint of these skills, men like Daddy could get what was due them after a day's work that threatened to wear them, their mules and their overalls out before their time.

And just like men, mules and overalls, the cloth cover on Daddy's old Bible was also over-worked and frazzled.

There was one Christmas when Susan and I gave him a new Bible, one that smelled like the seats in a new car.

The print was big and crisp on white, low mileage pages that had no dog ears on the corners or sparrow tracks between the columns.

"I like it," he said.

Yea! He liked it so much that he put it away for a rainy day revival, and I don't remember ever seeing it again.

He liked his old Bible. It continued to be his work horse when it came to plowing new and sometimes old ground. There he planted flowers for the Master's bouquet, just like it says in that old song Daddy used to sing in church.

Sometimes I wonder just how many miles his finger traveled along those pages. He'd track each word while that sixth finger of his anchored the page so a sneeze from the Devil wouldn't blow him off course. I can hear him now as his voice stumbled down each line, struggling to read "The Word" from atop a pulpit.

And believe you me, those pulpits were many and strung out from mosquito-infested nooks in North Florida to sacred shanties along red dirt roads in south Alabama.

Lord, how many miles did he and that Bible travel together?

How many dusty roads did they go down, only to find he'd turned at the first oak tree instead of the second one and ended up in a cornfield. Then he'd have to reach in his shirt pocket and pull out the mill pay stub he'd drawn the map on and backtrack like any good shepherd searching for his flock.

To get back on the right track, all he had to do was follow the sparrow tracks scribbled across the back of an old pay stub.

I could've had an easier time staying on track if I'd just had the faith to follow the sparrow tracks he left behind. Faith is a powerful thing. After all, even a sparrow needs a good dose of it when he makes that first jump off a limb.

For decades, Daddy and that Bible were inseparable. Except for maybe when he was at work at the mill—then he carried it in his heart.

And when death did separate him and that Bible and he fell to the bed that night, I'm sure it resonated in Heaven and God knew he had fallen.

Just like it says about the sparrow in Daddy's old Bible.

"Let the life you live be the sermon you preach."
—Billy Blackman

What If…

BUMPER THUMPER

SOMETIMES ON THE SLOW nights when no one was out dancing, my mind would wander and I would wonder what if, after decades of playing in bars and backing through life in the dark without tail lights to guide me, I got called to preach and follow in Daddy's footsteps—in his sparrow tracks.

What if…?

The tailgate on the Ford pickup was down and sagging under the weight of the Bible Thumper and his box of free pamphlets. He called them his "Get Out Of Hell Free" cards.

"DON'T GO IN THAT PLACE!"

Brother Bill was shouting with a Bible in one hand pointing up toward his reward. The fingers on his other hand were pointing toward the juke parking lot. Like five stubby gun barrels, they were aimed at people walking through the dust fog rising from the dirt lot as car loads of sinners slid to a stop in unmarked parking spots. Well, they were sorta marked by the size of the black circles on the dirt. Some oil pans leaked more than others.

The preacher would aim his fingers at five sinners at once.

"IF Y'ALL GOING IN THERE TO POUR YO'SELF A SIN AND TONIC, YOU NEED TO LET GOD BE THE TONIC."

Bill's daddy was a preacher who had polydactyly. That gave him a slight advantage over Bill because he could aim at six sinners at once, even with one hand tied behind his back.

It was sundown on Saturday. These working folks had bent their backs all week. Now they had a little cash and a lot of thrust.

But people don't always drink because they're thirsty. Some drink to forget—a 100-proof shot of amnesia for a life filled with bad decisions, backaches, heartbreaks, and sometimes just plain old bad luck.

"THE DEVIL LIVES IN THAT DEN OF SIN."

Brother Bill preached as the tailgate struggled to hold up this prophet and his box of pamphlets.

"THAT PLACE IS A TEMPLE OF TEMPTATION, A HAREM OF HARLOTS IN HIGH HEELS AND STRUMPETS STRUMMIN' ON OUT-OF-TUNE HEART STRINGS!"

The shocks squeaked under the truck bed. The Ford's back tires sagged with every downbeat as the "Thumper Over A Bumper" danced in the spirit across the tailgate.

"COME ON DOWN! IT'S TIME TO ALTER YOUR LIVES AT THIS ALTAR INSTEAD OF GOING IN THERE."

Brother Bill pointed at the Detroit-built altar under his feet, the one with F-O-R-D stamped on it.

"GOD DON'T CARE IF YA GOT WHISKEY ON YOUR BREATH. I DON'T EITHER! SO COME ON DOWN TO THE ALTAR, YE TROUBLED AND LOST SOULS!"

"Bill, I'm fine right here where I am," said a big voice from a man called Tiny.

Tiny Blanchard (his real name was Luke, but people called him"Tiny") had to squeeze to get across the juke's threshold. He bowed his head just enough to miss the door facing as he gazed back over his shoulder at his friend, Bill.

Legend told that he was so strong he once changed a flat tire on a loaded pulpwood truck and never used a jack. But you know how legends are. They grow best in low-light places, watered with alcohol and fertilized with exaggeration and bull manure.

The bar owner paid Tiny $50 a night to toss trouble makers out the door. But Tiny seldom had to scruff anybody across the threshold. One look at him and most of the time they volunteered to walk out on their own.

To Tiny, being a "lost soul" was not all that troubling if you're okay with where you are. Bouncing at "Donk's Tonk" is where he was, and that was okay with him.

The place was named "Donk's Tonk" because the owner, Hollis Collinsworth, had fists as fast, hard, and accurate as a donkey's kick. When you're in a confined space with only one door and that space is full of hardy guffaws and wannabe outlaws, hard fists are just part of a bar owner's standard equipment. That and a cell phone with the sheriff's department on speed dial.

It was only 8 o'clock, and the place was already half-full of Casanovas drinking Coors, some in various degrees of hygienic upkeep with mud on their boots and dirt on their minds.

The cars just kept coming, dusting their way into parking spots.

"It's gonna be a good night," Hollis thought to himself as he looked out the door at the rising dust cloud. With an occasional BIC flashing to light a cigarette, it reminded him of lightning in an approaching storm. But that was alright as long as it rained a little cash. Tiny would take care of the thunder and lightning.

He also saw Bill standing above them all, hollering out scriptures instead of Haggard's songs the way he used to from the stage inside Donk's Tonk.

"Why is it okay for Bill to give away church pamphlets in my parking lot, but not okay for me to give away liquor samples at his church picnic?" Hollis asked Tiny. He was afraid that the preacher might scare off the regulars.

Tiny shrugged his massive shoulders. That caused the bottom of his shirt to raise up and show that it was just his belly and not a beer keg he was trying to sneak in the door.

During his pre-preacher life, Bill had walked across hundreds of tonk parking lots toting a guitar case in his right hand and a dream of Nashville in his shirt pocket.

But even after being born again, he still has to admit that there is something melodic about the sound of a blond-ish/green-ish haired lady in high heels making her way across a graveled parking lot.

The one he's watching now has a lit cigarette in the right corner of her mouth and her right eye is squinting to keep the smoke out.

She's wearing an over-washed shirt with a faded picture of Porter Wagoner and Dolly Parton on the front. The caption reads "A Couple of Big'uns."

She's walking across that graveled lot heading for the front door. It's a steamy summer night where the air is so thick and damp that you can almost catch it in a jug and use it as a chaser.

She's in a pair of hot-red, high-heeled stilts she bought on sale somewhere inside somebody's garage.

The spikes on her heels are taking turns bogging and grinding through the gravel as she opens the dance hall door and a George Jones song falls out and hits the ground in a cloud of red clay dust mixed with grey, slightly used, low-mileage cigarette smoke.

She has on a white hat with a hatband made from a bolo tie her fourth husband told her he bought at a Roy Rogers estate sale in 1995. She didn't know that Roy Rogers didn't die until 1998. Her ex lied about a lot of stuff.

In the hatband, one feather sticks up. She said it's from some exotic bird. Everybody else thinks it came from the same crow that left his footprints around her eyes.

She's in a pair of red britches so tight that they look like they were painted on using a cheap brush bought at the Dollar Store. The brush marks are really just varicose veins and cellulite competing to see which can get through the cloth first.

She's wearing a fresh coat of matching red paint on her toe nails, her fingernails, her lips and her sashaying hips.

She steps inside as a moaning, haunting song originates from a stage held together with red carpet, dried beer and duct tape.

The karaoke singer is drunk again. He was once in a band that played here. But he was born again and now he's back again, tip-toeing through guitar cases in boots with no laces, dropping one-liners full of innuendos and guitar picks full of country licks.

On the dance floor, a former church lady is trying to teach a class a new square dance routine called "Backsliding." But the karaoke singer keeps stumbling over beer bottles and guitar cases and falling off the stage. Thank goodness the stage is only a cinder block plus plywood thickness from the floor.

The lady in the white hat and red britches winks at Tiny as she pays the cover charge because he said he liked her Roy Rogers hatband, then asked to see her ID.

Some guys just know the right things to say.

But Hollis need not worry about Bill running off business. If nothing else, he was part of the draw—the parking lot warm-up show for Amanda Lynn. She played a mandolin and went on at 9 with the "Single Barrel Band" making her sound good. They chose that name because of the amount of beer the band could consume in one night, and because none of them were married at the moment. But that could change—the night wasn't over yet and somebody's ex-husband could show up with a single barrel shotgun, again.

Sometimes a band's name has a good story to go with it.

The band almost got famous once while playing backup for an Elvis impersonator at a VFW in Odessa, Texas.

But then the law caught up with "Elvis" and arrested him for back child support. They ran the band out of the county—not because they were guilty of anything, but because they looked like they had to be guilty of something.

Their show at Donk's always started at 9 sharp and ended at 2 dull, after most of the regulars had staggered with Haggard on their breaths to the Waffle House to sit down, sop syrup and sober up.

Sin seemed to hide under every other table inside Donk's. Bill's mama used to tell him the Devil lay in wait under the tablecloth, ready to reach out and trip anybody who passed by too close. "Once you get up off the floor," she'd say, "you end up with red lipstick on your shirt collar and regret mixed in with yo grits the next moaning."

From experience, Bill knew she was right. Despite his mama's prayers, he had tripped and fallen inside that very building several times. It didn't involve lipstick and grits, but finger picks and playing his guitar under the neon light from a flashing beer sign. He was there chasing dreams like a dog chasing the band bus. And he was willing to chase it all the way to Nashville, if he didn't trip up and get run over in the process.

He was only going to play long enough to see if he could do something besides slinging a chainsaw and a spike maul. He figured it wouldn't take long to find that out. So he stepped across the Donk's threshold with his guitar in tow and just never seemed to come out again. That is, until that fateful night when he was "washed in the blood." That's a Southern euphemism for being "born again" by going down front at a local tent revival and "finding the Lord."

There comes a point when most folks prefer the taste of Sunday morning biscuits over the aftertaste of stale cigarette smoke and beer belches. For several years, Bill had been edging toward that point, dragging with him unrealized dreams and scarred lungs.

He was almost too far gone. His eyes were dark and lifeless, like raisin eyes on a crumbling gingerbread man. His mouth was set in a cracked, straight line against his red face. It looked like a split in a tomato that was too ripe or maybe just taken in too much liquid.

Bill was spending every night around people who saw themselves as professional drunks because they could stagger in a straight line walking home past the police station. But they were just plain ole drunks, singing and wobbling their way through life without knowing the words to the song. They weren't concerned about whose door facing they leaned against, whose toes they stepped on, or how many ex-wives they left back home.

Bill didn't fight what fate had handed him, he just accepted it as dues to be paid while his prayers to be a professional musician were being answered. It just seemed that God was taking His dear sweet time about it.

It had got to where the only time he ever prayed was at the end of the night when Hollis wrote the band a check. Bill would always throw the check on top of the bar in front of Hollis. "I'm just check'n to see if it'll bounce." Onlookers thought it was a joke. But from experience, Bill and Hollis knew it wasn't.

Then one fateful night after last call inside, Bill was crawling around on the floor with a table candle in his hand.

"Bill, what'cha doin'?" Tiny asked.

"Lookin' for my damn car keys," Bill said, looking up from the floor as Tiny towered over him. "I think I might need'a ride home."

"Come on," Tiny said. "I'll give you a lift."

A mile down the road, Tiny's overloaded little truck sputtered twice, then went dead. Unlike the driver or the passenger, the Ford Ranger was out of gas.

AA or Triple A could have helped them, but they had no way to call. Back then, the only cell phone they knew of was the one hanging on the wall at the county jail.

They coasted as far as they could. The truck stopped rolling in front of a patched circus tent pitched next to the road. Streaks of light and the sounds of hand claps, hallelujahs and smoke escaped through the tent flaps.

The tent had been there for a week. Bill knew what was going on because he'd been to several such gatherings with his preacher daddy. Tiny knew, too. To him, the light and noise inside the old circus tent was nothing more than a homing device that drew clowns like candle flies to a porch light.

Even at 2 a.m. the tent overflowed with what Tiny called "the foot washers and holy rollers." These were the teetotaler worshippers who took their religion without a chaser or time clock. They shouted and hollered and had a high ole time singing the ole time hymns as a hoarse, sweaty preacher screamed over a crackling microphone, showering the crowd like a thunderstorm, soaking them in that old time gospel.

"WHISKEY WON'T GIVE YOU THE ABILITY TO WALK ON WATER LIKE JESUS DID." The crackling voice bounced around the tent before escaping through the flaps.

"BUT IT CAN SHORE MAKE YOU THINK YOU DOIN' IT—RIGHT BEFORE YOU SINK TO THE BOTTOM!"

Bill wanted to go inside.

"I gotta get away from these sketters," he said as he slapped the side of his neck.

Smoke pots inside the tent had chased the hungry mosquitoes back outside where the two men were standing. It didn't seem to bother the mosquitoes that Bill and Tiny's blood was thinned and tainted with alcohol. Thin blood is better than no blood to a squadron of hungry mosquitoes that's not worried about having to fly home in a straight line. So, they swarmed Bill and Tiny, forcing them to open the tent flap to retreat into the smoke.

Fifteen minutes passed before the preacher did what preachers do—give the altar call at half volume.

"If any of y'all are tired of treading water to keep from drowning in sin, come on down front here. God is giving swimming lessons."

Tiny walked back toward the tent flap where he'd come in, grumbling something about circus clowns. But Bill was running in the other direction. He was ready to get his feet wet. After all the years of treading in smoky bars, Bill was ready to let Jesus give him swimming lessons inside a smoky tent.

Once he got to the front, Bill dropped to his knees into the sawdust, and this time he wasn't holding a candle and looking for his car keys. He was searching for something else. With whiskey on his breath, he was drawn down front by another light, seeking forgiveness and ready to be washed in the blood.

And like his daddy whose life changed after he had tracked through the sawdust inside that tent pitched on the ball field in St. Joe, Bill's life changed that night.

"If you don't think God answers your mama's prayers, just ask this sinner who lost his car keys and found his soul," Bill preached from his own pulpit a year later. He liked to preach about that night to his flock at the New Light Pentecostal Holiness Church, them throwing nods and amens at him because they didn't have many dollars to throw. But Bill didn't care about the money. It was the Lord's work.

"I have a new home now," he told his flock. "My old home had a dirt parking lot. The parking lot at my new home is paved in gold. I finally figured out that if God had really wanted me to play music so people could get drunk and fly high, He would'a put wings on bar stools and wouldn't'a put that verse in the Bible, 'Lo, I am with you always'."

His flock always laughed, no matter how many times they heard him say it on Sunday mornings.

And on Saturday nights, he'd preach the same thing from the tailgate of his truck in the parking lot of the ole juke joint where he had once attended religiously.

"You just never can tell," he'd explained when asked why he did it. "Some future Bible Thumper might be on his knees inside that juke right now, crawling around with a candle in his hand, searching for his car keys. And what if he needs a ride home!"

Made in the USA
Middletown, DE
27 July 2024

58054996R00229